Praise for
Shifting Sands:

Jewish Women Confront the Israeli Occupation

"Throughout history, women's stories have played a key role in drawing attention to social injustices and human rights violations. Indeed it is stories that have shaped the Jewish-American experience and collective memory. Yet, amid stories of suffering and triumph, so many nations, races, borders and "enemies" have been defined, that it demands the grueling work of unlearning preconceived notions in order to uncover the other stories that parallel these. This anthology contains Jewish-American women's stories spanning generations, life experiences, and means of questioning the status quo and making room for more than one victim. Their bravery in speaking out against the injustices perpetuated by our own people (this time) is not the main story here – the legacy they will create is through their acts of witnessing the truth, swallowing its ramifications and exposing stories too often untold to Jews worldwide. If there is ever to be true, just peace and reconciliation in Israel/Palestine, it must start with embracing our traditions and stories enough to depart from them and teach new ones."

Emily W. Schaeffer,
American-Israeli human rights lawyer and anti-occupation activist

"I applaud Osie Gabriel Adelfang and all those who contributed essays to *Shifting Sands*. Jews, and in particular Jewish women, are the natural force to be in the forefront of the efforts to end Israeli occupation of Palestinian lands, lives and future. From the opening pages about a Jewish prayer on doubt, through each and every one of the personal accounts, readers feel the wisdom of women on every page, as well as a deep sense of love for humanity—all humanity. *Shifting Sands* meticulously weaves the daily trials and tribulations of a military occupation with stories of real people who are dispossessed and subjected to daily doses of ethnic cleansing by a state drunk on power. Bottom line: the sands are truly shifting and this occupation is coming tumbling down, like all the other that came before it. When all is said and done, the women in this book—side by side with Palestinian women from Gaza, Jerusalem and Nablus—will form the foundation of a new Palestine and Israel that will flourish as one."

Sam Bahour,
Co-Editor of Homeland: Oral Histories of Palestine and Palestinians, *and Palestinian-American businessman in El-Bireh, occupied Palestine*

"This is a moving collection of readings by Jewish women writers who are committed to the quest for justice and compassion in Palestine and Israel. They powerfully articulate, in their different ways, the axiom of our common humanity. It may have taken our whole life to reach that place (as one contributor put it), but those who are finally able to see, must stand up and advocate for sanity now, today."

Deb Reich,
translator, Abu Ghosh, Israel/Palestine

"Writing with personal modesty yet great humanity, these courageous women offer richly textured, revelatory accounts that will grip the reader's thoughts and feelings. All the selections are finely rendered, insightful, and endowed with a determined sense of justice and compassion."

Michael Parenti,
author of Contrary Notions *and* God and His Demons

shifting sands

Jewish Women Confront
the Israeli Occupation

**EDITED
BY** Osie
Gabriel
Adelfang

WHOLE WORLD PRESS

WHOLE WORLD PRESS
14150 NE 20th Street F1, #305
Bellevue, WA 98007
www.wholeworldpress.org

Special discounts for bulk purchases are available. Please contact Whole World Press at
bulksales@wholeworldpress.org for more information.

Cover Credits:
Collage by Mim Golub Scalin
Cover photos by Susan Greene, Dalit Baum, Eric Drooker
Vintage b/w photo (cover): photographer unknown, courtesy of the editor
Graphic Design by Barbara Hodge

Interior Credits:
"Cherish Your Doubts" by Robert T. Weston and first published by Beacon Press in
Hymns for the Celebration of Live (c) 1964
Appendices I, III, V by Anna Baltzer
Graphic Design by Barbara Hodge

Shifting Sands: Jewish Women Confront the Israeli Occupation / edited by
Osie Gabriel Adelfang
Includes bibliographical references and maps
ISBN: 978-0-9845128-1-2
Library of Congress Control Number: 2010927204

Additional Note:
Whole World Press does not have any control over and does not assume any responsibility for author or third-party Web sites or their content.

Dedication:

For my father, who taught by example that you can and should
stand up to authority against injustice. I hope he would be proud.
And to the memories of my babies, Erika and Noah, who never got to
experience the challenges and joys of living on this earth.

Table of Contents

Preface

Amira Hass

There's a Jewish joke that goes: At the end of the 19th Century, a Jewish mother in Czarist Russia is getting her son ready to go off to the war that has again erupted between Russia and Turkey. She is organizing his knapsack and meanwhile is scared to death for his safety. "Moishele" (or "Shloimele," it makes no difference), she says to him; "when you get to the front—kill a Turk and take a break; kill a Turk, and take a break."

"But Mom," replies Moishele (or Shloimele, it makes no difference), "what will happen if, while I am taking a break, a Turk kills me?"

"*Oy vey iz mir!*"—exclaims his mother—"What would a Turk have against you?!"

"Kill a Turk and take a break" is today an Israeli expression meaning "don't rush, take it easy." Those who use it as an innocent idiom choose to ignore its intrinsic violence. In Israel, the original subversive and self-critical implications of this Jewish joke, so poignant, have been erased.

Yet in this very Israel, during the past five or six years, hundreds of Israelis have participated, and continue to participate, in demonstrations against the Separation Wall. They frequently try to intervene between Palestinians and the army, as the army aims at dispersing Palestinian demonstrators by any available means. The local folklore attributes to some young Palestinian demonstrators the following description of the situation:

"On one side stood the Jews"—sadly, that means the army, or the repressive regime—"shooting stun grenades, tear gas, rubber-coated metal bullets; and on the other side, the Israelis come and shout at the Jews to get out of there and stop shooting at unarmed demonstrators."

"These are not the Jews we have known," I heard from Gazans a few days after the end of the massive Israeli military onslaught on Gaza in winter 2008-2009. Among those talking with me were people whose loved ones had been killed by soldiers—children and women and old people—at close range. Others had had their homes or fields destroyed, and sometimes both. All had lived through three weeks of terror that is beyond description. Again, "the Jews" meant the army, (and the speakers compared the recent unfettered violence to what they now interpret as the army's restraint during the first Intifada). But they were also thinking of ordinary Jews—civilians they had met in Israel, back when they were able to get out of Gaza to go there.

"My (Jewish) former employer was the first to send me money when he heard that my house had been destroyed—before Hamas, before the Palestinian Authority," several people told me when they realized I was Israeli. They had known the "other" Jews, before the Israeli policy of separation made it impossible for Palestinians to enter Israel, make friends with Israeli Jews, and interact with them as human beings, not only as representatives of the occupation.

Since the beginning of the 1990s, in tandem with what is known as "the peace process," successive Israeli governments have promoted "separation" as a moral and administrative ideal: separation between Jews and Palestinians, between Palestinians and Palestinians.

In the Orwellian lexicon that has developed during recent years, Peace is Separation. Small wonder that the only Israeli-Jews the younger generations of Palestinians know are settlers and soldiers.

Meanwhile, there are Israeli Jews engaged in dozens of diverse and ongoing activities against the occupation. They are, regretfully, a very small minority, but they do defy the separation and break down walls, both literally and symbolically.

The writings in this anthology take their place as part of this "other" Jewish tradition, the tradition of those who tell jokes and break down walls.

Ramallah, October 20, 2009
Translated by Deb Reich

Foreword

Cindy Sheehan

In 1999, I was offered an opportunity to travel to Israel on a tour sponsored by my Catholic parish. Having grown up very poor in a working-class suburb of Los Angeles, I had never even traveled much outside Southern California. The idea of going to this ancient land was exciting but frightening, because from what I knew through the US media (what most Americans who get their information about the Middle East from the media "know"), was that the area was dangerous, with leaders like Yasser Arafat, PLO sponsored terrorism, and frequent suicide bombings of innocent civilians. There was a chance I'd be a victim of this widespread violence. However, I was an ardent Catholic at the time, so the chance to see the land's holy sites and walk in the footsteps of Jesus won out over fear. I applied for my first passport ever, and went.

The Holy Land was almost exactly as I'd pictured it, and I felt completely secure as I waded in the warm waters of the Mediterranean and the iffy waters of the Jordan River, interacting with our tour guide and other Israelis. But having been taught to fear Palestinians, I was still somewhat worried about the next leg of our trip, viewing the landscape of Jesus' life. But then, from Bethlehem to Bethany to the ancient city of

Jericho, I was astonished at the kindness of the Palestinians I met, who welcomed our group with open arms and open hearts.

I never met a mean or rude person in these (in 1999) Palestinian areas. On the other hand, when a Palestinian woman holding a dirty, sick child begged me for Shekels in Jerusalem, our Israeli tour guide scolded me: "You are being too free with your money to the 'dogs.'" As I shed my misconceptions and saw the truth of the situation, my heart began to melt with compassion for the oppressed people of Palestine.

Two years later, when the US was attacked on 9/11, my first inclination was to wonder: What would make a person take his own life and the lives of others in such a terrible way? As inexcusable and horrific as flying airplanes into buildings and killing thousands is, in terms of impact on our powerful nation, these attackers were no more successful than the Palestinian teen throwing a rock at an Israeli Defense Force (IDF) soldier in the West Bank or the Qassam rockets fired from blockaded Gaza into Israel. Why do it? Did they feel like they had no other choice of action, no hope for their futures, no other way to be free?

Our country reacted in fear as Israel reacts: using immense force against a weak opponent. We invaded Iraq in 2003, and my son Casey—a soldier of our occupying army—was killed there in 2004. In honor of his life and of all human life, I began to speak out. First, I spoke against the occupation of Iraq, then of Afghanistan, then of Palestine. To me, it's an American issue just like the others: without our country's extensive financial and "moral" support, Israel could not continue to do what it does.

When the Biblical Moses came down from Mount Ararat with two stone tablets, he presented us with God's ten most basic commandments. One is so self-evident, so apparent, that it requires no further explanation: "Thou shalt not kill." There were no caveats or codicils to this commandment. God did not give any wiggle room.

For speaking out, I was (and am) called "anti-American" and "anti-Semitic." I am neither. To say that I am anti-American is to say that I hate myself, my children, my parents, and my friends. That is not true. To be anti-Semitic means that I hate both Jews and Palestinians (I hate neither). I am "anti immoral occupations" and opposed to the governments that perpetrate and perpetuate them. Or, more to the point, I am pro-peace, pro-justice, pro-human-rights. So it is that the 14 brave women who contributed to this important collection will undoubtedly be called anti-Semitic (or rather, self-hating). I instead put us all in the category of loving humanity, no matter what walls (real or imagined) separate us.

I am proud to write the introduction to this collection of essays and poetry by 14 brilliant Jewish women. Here, they share their lives and wisdom with us, so we can better understand the rejection of the oppressor and the embracing of the oppressed. Through these histories and testimonials, we are taken to a human world where transformation comes early or late, but it always comes. We are privileged to witness such grace.

Cherish your doubts, for doubt is the handmaiden of truth.

Doubt is the key to the door of knowledge.

It is the servant of discovery.

A belief which may not be questioned binds us to error,
for there is incompleteness and imperfection in every belief.

Doubt is the touchstone of truth.

It is an acid which eats away the false.

Let none fear for the truth, that doubt may consume it;
for doubt is a testing of belief.

For truth, if it be truth, arises from each testing stronger, more secure.

Those who would silence doubt are filled with fear.

The house of their spirit is built on shifting sands.

But they that fear not doubt, and know its use, are founded on a rock.

They shall walk in the light of growing knowledge.

The work of their hands shall endure.

Therefore, let us not fear doubt, but let us rejoice in its help;
it is to the wise as a staff to the blind.

Doubt is the handmaiden of truth.

Lights Vanish from Lifta

By Linda Dittmar

My parents, sister, and I are packed into a tiny pale blue van traveling for a long-awaited day at the beach. On weekdays, the van is my dad's company vehicle for hauling and repairing machines, but it is our family car for the weekend. In those years immediately following Israel's War of Independence, we are privileged to have use of any vehicle at all. In the van with us are a picnic lunch, bathing suits, sun cream and hats. We're headed to the small, shimmering, rocky bays at Tantura, driving north from Tel Aviv. Just before the turnoff from the main coastal highway, we pass a sprawling Arab village, its houses creeping up the Carmel Mountain's slope. Later, I learn that the village is called Fureidis. Fureidis, so the story goes, got its name from an English traveler who was so taken with its beauty that he called it "paradise," though all I see from the car is the flat dirt stretch that extends between that rise and the coastal road on which we are driving.

A large, ramshackle shantytown has materialized to hold my 12-year-old gaze. Everything seems caked with reddish earth and dry grime—the patched up tents, the makeshift lean-tos of recycled corrugated tin and assorted boards, and the raggedy children who stare at us as we drive by. I stare back at them, children my age and younger, at once familiar and yet utterly alien. Flies are everywhere, buzzing around the children, landing on their faces... My parents avert their eyes; we are silent.

To get to the beach we turn west, away from Fureidis. The van crosses a flat plane and climbs over a rise before it reaches the beach. Along this crest are remnants of walls; the dusty remains of stone houses crumble and blend back into sand dunes. Succulent plants somehow manage to grow on the dunes. Here and there are some prickly pear bushes and an occasional date tree. Only some 40 years later do I learn to "read" the landscape: in Israel any fruit-tree that seems to be growing wild, and the prickly pear most commonly, is a marker, a sign of previous Palestinian habitation. Someone planted it and willed it to live. But my sister and I are restless, thinking only of the beach ahead. For us, the remnants of stone walls, the cactus, and the date trees are just a landscape we take for granted. Hot and sticky, we are eager to finally squeeze out of the van's storage area, where we've been bumping on the metal floor.

We stake our little patch of beach territory with towels, bags, and the beach umbrella under which our mother hides from the sun. I scramble on the ruins to explore them. I feel the heat under my bare feet and the roughness of the stones as I grasp them to keep from falling. Later, I will find myself a rock away from the family, where I daydream between swims. But now I am on the move, as I have also been on other occasions in near-by Caesarea (the Arab Barrat Qisarya), where I groped my way up the dark narrow steps spiraling inside the abandoned village minaret. This was before Qisarya was turned into a major tourist destination, before the minaret's low opening into the tiny Muezzin's balcony, way up high, got walled in with concrete.

It never occurred to me in those days to wonder why Quisarya's minaret was available for climbing, or why huddled near it were a few abandoned stone buildings with sweeping arches. Like Fureidis' refugee camp or the prickly pears closer to the sea, Quisarya's ruins were naturalized as part of the landscape. Very briefly, this is what I learned since:

Tantura is one of about 400 Palestinian villages (estimates range from 350 to 450 or even 500) destroyed during Israel's War of Independence in 1948.

Archival photographs document the expulsion of Tantura's residents, many of whom camped in nearby Fureidis before being expelled to Arab-held lands. (Fureidis may have been spared because of its close ties with Jewish Zichron Yaakov.) Jewish Dor and Kibbutz Nakhsholim, both on Tantura's lands, each manage its own resort. A 19th century glass factory and an archaeological dig further blur the centuries-old Palestinian presence. The nearby fishing village of Barrat Qisarya (Caesarea), also forcibly evacuated, is now a major archaeological site (Roman, Herodian, and Crusader), a beach resort, and one of Israel's most exclusive communities. Its restored Roman amphitheater hosts popular international concerts. A short detour at the entrance to Dor leads to a memorial to the Alexandroni Brigade that "liberated" Tantura. Recent research suggests that a massacre occurred during the villagers' expulsion.

* * *

In the years before Israel became a state, my family often travels in a stuffy collective taxi to visit my grandmother in the Jewish Jerusalem suburb of Beit Hakerem. A few kilometers west of Jerusalem, we pass the Palestinian village of Lifta, facing westward just as we enter the city. I know we are reaching Lifta when two small coffee shops appear on the left, close by the roadside, with low rush-seat stools clustered on their small concrete platforms as if perching over a precipice. The village itself appears next, descending to the valley below. As we drive, the first houses of the Romema neighborhood rise above Lifta, facing the Jewish Yeshivas. Beit Hakerem can't be far. I love craning my neck to see Lifta down below, its seemingly tiny stone houses nestled peacefully into the mountainside. In February, the almonds bloom. At dusk, faint lights can be seen in some windows. The young child I am before the war imagines people going about their evening chores there, much like my grandmother. She, Savta, would turn off the kerosene cooker, wash and stack dishes, and prepare for bed, her shoes click-clacking back and forth on the stone floor. Her feet were always swollen and hurting, as are those of many older women in our difficult climate, Jewish and Arab alike. As night falls Lifta, like my grandmother's home, seems blanketed in safety.

During the War of Independence, we can't go to Jerusalem. The city is under siege, with Savta on the other side. Eventually, she gets out in an armored vehicle caravan traveling the makeshift "Burma Road," built surreptitiously behind enemy lines. The fighting is finally over as I turn eleven.

When we can travel to Beit Hakerem once again, I notice that there are no lights in Lifta. In daytime we no longer hear from Savta's patio Lifta's men calling "*barroud... barroud...*," their voices rising from the nearby quarry as they prepare to dynamite new rock. I used to be endlessly fascinated by this call, as *barroud* is a sister-word to *barrad*, Hebrew for hail. Now, after the war, my grandmother no longer haggles with the Arab women who would bring apricots or figs for sale, carrying them in large flat baskets balanced on their head. There had always been at least two, sometimes three women, wearing long, black, lavishly embroidered dresses. They would all sit cross-legged on the cool stone patio of Savta's semi-basement apartment. She would hold up a fig in late summer, pointing out in Arabic a barely noticeable blemish, while they would praise its freshness. And so it went, at leisure, till Savta amassed a small mound and the women would amble off – to the next house? To Lifta? To the nearby Palestinian village of Deir Yassin?

On a later trip, I notice a few electric lights in Lifta's small windows. The new lights are brighter but sparser. Before the war, many more windows glowed, even if less distinctly. I miss the companionable crowding of those dimmer lights (kerosene, as I later learn), now replaced by those occasional bursts of harsh electricity.

Later still, darkness returns.

I was drawn to the dimmer lights and am uneasy when they are gone. There was something unsettling about the ominous darkness that descended on the village, as if inexplicably, and something puzzling about the harsh light's appearance. I don't understand those changes. No-one comments, and I never ask. In daylight, the distant village seems unchanged. In summer, Savta and I sit in her patio sorting lentils as we always have.

To this day, when I take the bus to Jerusalem, I always choose the left side so I can see Lifta. Yet only recently have I registered consciously how few houses remain. The occasional new electric lights tell me that the village is being repopulated—by squatters, as it turns out, and by a group of orthodox Jews who use the small reservoir for bathing. A hiking trail passes through the lower part of the village, where the water has recently been channeled to make for a pleasant shady path. But higher up, the almonds trees are infested and dying. The abandoned houses are falling apart, their domed roofs caving in, their walls gradually disintegrating as mortar gives way to cracks.

Plans to incorporate the surviving buildings into an upscale Jewish suburb are now underway. The village of my imagination remains a pastoral landscape. A tiny woman here, a man riding a donkey there, or a few children playing among domed houses may be visible far off in the Lifta of my memory. This pastoral Lifta is also, most crucially, the Edenic village of the Palestinians' imagination. It is the landscape inhabited by them for millennia. It is also the landscape cherished by the early Jewish settlers of Eretz Yisrael from the last decades of the 19th century to the early decades of the 20th.

Lifta, overlooking the crucial Western entrance to Jerusalem, was captured early on in the war, after an attack on the roadside coffee shop where several patrons were killed. Though its residents fled and many of its houses were destroyed, seen at a distance the village retains its charm. The electric power dates to a failed attempt to resettle it with Jewish immigrants. In 1987 the Israeli Nature Reserves Authority considered turning Lifta into an open air museum that would "stress the Jewish roots of the site." This role was eventually assigned to another village, Sataf, which may have less real estate potential because it is further away from Jerusalem. Sataf is now a well-developed tourist site modeling "Biblical" agriculture with well-tended terrace farming, water sources, and hiking trails. Deir Yassin, referred to briefly above, is the site of the most notorious massacre of Palestinians during the war of 1948. Its infamy spread among the Palestinians and spurred the flight of many. Scores of people perished.

* * *

It is cold and dreary on that winter day in 1949 when my uncle takes us, cousins ranging in age from 11 to 16, on a trip south to the Negev. The earth is muddy and steel-gray rain clouds are hanging low. A clammy dampness penetrates our clothes, but all around us the land is finally, after months without rain, freshly green. I am barely 11 and don't know much about the war beyond what filters in at home: air raids, bomb shelters and sandbags, tape crisscrossing glass windows, mom volunteering at a military hospital, dad off on guard duty in his baggy uniform, and those occasions when mother, Savta, and I are in the kitchen, boiling and re-rolling bandages for the hospital. I don't yet read the paper, but I gleaned enough from radio broadcasts and grown-up conversations to know that my uncle is taking us to visit key areas of combat—places whose names have a special aura: al-Falouja, Iraq al-Manshiya, Yad Mordechai, Iraq Suwaydan... places that saw heavy fighting, where "our fighters" emerged victorious against great odds.

The front façade of the former British police station of Iraq Suwaydan is pockmarked with bullets holes. This fortified police station is one of a string of such British forts that guard major arteries and are readily identifiable by their template architecture and ochre color. Its capture by Israeli forces is yet another testimonial to our valor and to the justice of our cause. The fact that we are at these battlefields by special permission, at a time when civilians are not yet allowed into the combat zone, makes us feel powerful. We seem to share the adrenaline flow of the young men (and women) who were fighting for our lands and future. We pause to absorb the sight, staring at the bullet-riddled wall with awe, aware that live mines may still be nearby.

As we follow the ruts made in dirt roads by Jeeps and other military vehicles, we pass nameless Palestinian villages where roofs are already caving in and mud-brick walls are beginning to give way under the pounding force of the season's semi-tropical rains. New grass is already sprouting on whatever is left of the collapsed buildings. The grass is a bright emerald color, exuberantly affirming the return of life against the background of this destruction. We stare as we drive by, but don't comment. We think of Yad Mordechai, founded by Warsaw Ghetto fighters who now bravely resisted Egyptian attack, the few against the many. We think of Iraq Suwaydan's bullet-riddled wall and the "boys" who fell there, heroically sacrificing their lives for the young nation that is coming into being. We, whose young state rests on their sacrifice, feel strong, proud, and capable. This, after all, was the point of the expedition. I am wishing I were old enough to die for my country, like Josef Trumpeldor, whose dying words defending Tel Chai every school child learns with reverence: *Tov lamut be'ad artzeino* (It is good to die for our country).

But I also sense intuitively, without deliberate thought, the ironies of what is before us: the senses' pleasure at nature's renewal—the life-giving rain, the grass, even the chill in the air—but also a barely understood aware-ness that this particular renewal feeds on the dying body of what was a living village. Some 40 years later I find myself reading Isaac Diqs' memoir, *A Bedouin Boyhood*. The book recounts its author's life in that same region, including his being sent to boarding school in the regional capital of Beersheba (now Be'er Sheva) just before the 1948 war began. Home for vacation, he finds that the entire tribe has decamped. All that remains are circles of cinders marking the household campfires and abandoned dogs foraging for food. Diqs and I were both about 10 years old at the time.

Fast-forward 25 years to Ariela Azulai's photo exhibition, *Ma'aseh Medina* ("The Story of a State" at the Zochrot gallery, Tel Aviv, April-May 2009, now published by Resling, Israel). Among the photographs on display are several documenting the depopulation of the Negev immedi-ately preceding that dreary morning of my visit. In these mostly journal-istic images, culled from diverse archives, I once again find the Negev I saw 60 years ago. It is again overcast. The earth is still rutted and muddy. Soldiers are wearing their scratchy dark khaki woolen battledress jackets. In one picture we see a donkey, still tethered, standing patiently in an abandoned courtyard; through an open door one can see kitchen utensils left helter-skelter in the room. Another picture shows three Palestinian men facing the camera, one of them an elderly dignitary. The caption tells us that he is here to talk with the Israeli commander, confident that his village will be spared because of its good relations with its Jewish neighbors. That old chill penetrates my bones once again.

The battlegrounds of the Negev had an iconic stature in the annals of Israel's War of Independence. Al-Falouja—a hill top village bordered by a deep wadi—had a commanding view of major highways. The police fort of Iraq

Suwaydan, also strategically placed and held by the invading Egyptian army, was only captured after eight failed Israeli attempts. All in all, fighting in the Falouja "pocket" was fierce, as Israelis battled both an Egyptian brigade and Palestinians. In counterweight to these sites of conquest, Yad Mordechai, the coda to our tour of Negev battlegrounds, is an icon of Zionist aspirations. Barely a mile north of the Gaza, and named for Mordechai Analevicz, the 22-year-old leader of the Warsaw Ghetto uprising, this kibbutz echoes Tel Chai's heroic account of Jewish pioneers/defenders who make the desert bloom and put the good of the many ahead of individual survival.

* * *

The woman I am today tries to touch the baffled child she was 60 years ago—a child half-paralyzed by an unvoiced prohibition against naming what she sees, let alone questioning it. On the cusp of adolescence, old enough to remember, to wonder, to sense the meanings of what she sees and what is left unsaid, she is complicit in the silences around her. Even at a young age she knows enough to turn her back on the self-evident—on the stunned gaze of the children standing listlessly in Fureidis' make-shift slum, the lights that vanish from Lifta, the young grass that sprouts on clay houses as they melt in the winter rains. What haunts me today is the sense that this child did know, understand, and question more than she allowed herself to register. Poised on a threshold, she had a choice between recognition and complicity. It is this choice that I am striving to understand today—not only that child's but the choice all of us adults have as we face the inchoate, liminal and ultimately transgressive call to speak up.

The child I was lived under a pall that may partly account for the silence in which everybody around her colluded. There was the literal pall of blackout curtains to protect against bombings and the dash to shelters whenever a siren went off. There was also the intangible pall of daily life in time of war: the air-raids and the explosions that shook the walls; photographs of the bright-faced young people who became the "fallen"; the abandoned Arab dogs that strayed into the city and were left for dead one morning as children headed for school; and the insistent radio program, broadcast several times daily at the end of the news, "Mi Makir, Mi Yode'a" ("Who recognizes/Who Knows"):

> *"Rachel Goldberg of Kibbutz Hazore'a is looking for her cousin Rivke Brunovsky of Julnitz... Yitzhak Smilovitz, originally from Kiev, now living in Hadera, is looking for Bettye Smilovitz, daughter of Rivka and Reb Yisruel... Grisha Dinovsky of Gdansk is looking for his brother, Abrasha... Esther and Moyshe Gvirtz are looking for... Dunya Appleman is looking... Hayka Lichtinov is looking..."*

The litany seemed unending: people searching or being searched for by loving relatives and friends who may or may not have perished in the Holocaust, who may or may not have immigrated to Israel, who may or may not be listening to the program at that particular hour. As Jewish refugees flowed into Israel, with their strange accents and concentration camp numbers tattooed on their arms, with their desperate hold on a tenuous life, there was no escaping the emotions this ritual reading stirred up several times each day.

Beyond the boundless horror we had to repress, suspend, and deny lay a profoundly self-repudiating shame at the powerlessness and degradation marking so many of "us"—our people. This fusing of terror, mourning, and shame is not tangential to that other silence about "them"—the Palestinians. We were all caught up in lies and denials that we deeply believed, and still do, as essential to our raw survival. The little girl I was could not escape a world where ethics and self-interest collide. Though the miasma that enveloped that world was not of her making, she could not help being complicit in it. Inevitably, her numbness was woven into the invisible fabric of the collective mystification that accounts for the Israel we now have.

As I attempt to understand my own footprints in this blood-soaked land, that numbness threatens to return—except that now, at age 70, I am more ready to resist it. I can let memory fragments surface, even if already altered by the wishes and inhibitions that inevitably recast what we know of the past. Something stirs, a will to give shape to the inchoate mess that my point of origin—my relation to the founding of a Jewish state and the Palestinian calamity that made it possible. Living with both the colonizing "Original Sin" of Zionism and the "Never Again" heritage of Jewish suffering, there was no telling where I'd turn. For many years, the *Nakbah* was only on the periphery of my vision. Like many others, I went on with my life without fully understanding where I had been or where I was heading. But change does occur, even if imperceptibly.

There is really no "right" moment for change, and no clear path. Mine was gradual, circuitous, and cumulative. What insights I gained were barely recognizable as "insights" at the time. As I search for a key moment, that dramatic turning point, only fragments surface. While none can be called a turning point, the "afterimage" each left persists and blends with others. Among them is the massacre at Kfer Qassim (1956), where Israeli soldiers obeyed orders to kill Palestinian farmers, including women, returning home after curfew. Included also, miles away, is my chancing on the leveled Armenian city of old Van in eastern Turkey, so evocative of the Negev ruins of my childhood. At work, finally, is all I have also learned here, in the United States, as my horizon expanded to include a broader understanding of ways global and local struggle find points of contact around race, gender, class, colonization, and much more.

With this awareness honed over many years, it was not much of a leap for me to recoil from Ariel Sharon's belligerent "peace visit," as he called it, to Jerusalem's Haram a-Sharif (Temple Mount), accompanied by some 1,000 "guards" in uniform. In themselves, the arrogance, complacency, and swaggering bravado of that deliberately provocative move did not amount to a revelation. I grew up with this Israeli brand of flexed muscles that tries in vain to disguise—if not heal—the collective trauma accumulated over two millennia's worth of abjectness. But the blatant glee with which Sharon indulged in this particular show of strength was more than I could bear. Its evident excess made it morally urgent for me to redirect my energies towards my point of origin.

The protective shield of numbness in which I had encased myself began to buckle under the weight of facts I could no longer ignore: riots at Joseph's Tomb; the first Intifada and then the second; the brutality of the separation wall and closures; Jewish settlers uprooting olive trees and decimating crops; and now the most recent siege on Gaza which, for all its spectacular force and large scale devastation, is hardly unprecedented.

Though Sharon's utter disdain for Palestinian feelings triggered in me a particularly intense moral outrage, it is important for me to register that this response did not come to me in a flash. It crept and sidled towards me; it coaxed, bullied, and shamed me. But in the process, in ways that will always be somewhat mysterious, something did change, as it does for many of us who change without being able to account for it. At some point it became impossible for me to continue blinding myself to the direction Israel has been taking. Pried loose, I became free to question what I had taken for immutable truths: the myth of the land waiting for redemption, the conviction that this land was ordained to be ours, the pride in the decency and humanity of our fighting forces... It is a circuitous journey that leads many of us toward a new awareness that reconciliation and peace must stand on the bedrock of truth.

Okupacia

By Maia Ettinger

In Poland, where we lived till I was five, the Second World War was on everyone's mind. My mother was Jewish, some of her friends were Jewish, and many were not. The Jews had lost nearly everyone, the Gentiles more than a few, and all of them had lived through the war. They called it The Occupation. Even today, when I talk to my relatives in Warsaw on the phone, that's what we call it: *Okupacia*.

After my mother and I came to the United States, Americans would exclaim: "how lucky you are, getting out of Poland!" This inevitably ignited my mother's simmering fury. She did not feel lucky; she felt exiled. In 1968, Poland targeted its surviving Jews with a campaign of anti-Semitism meant to distract a restive populace from its grievances against the state. Even Communist Party members like my mother were induced to leave the country. She had spent her 13th birthday in the Warsaw Ghetto, and her 40th in a basement interrogation room with the Polish secret police, but my mother left her homeland reluctantly. Post-war Poles understood each other; volatile rage, reflexive secrecy, and bull-headed obstinacy were practically the national code of conduct. She never fully made peace with her new life among credulous smiling people who had never known war.

A few years after we arrived, we got a coffee-table book about the Six Day War called *Lightening Out of Israel*, and Moshe Dayan became my hero. He looked as I imagined the entire Israeli military to be: brave, dashing and honorable. A dispenser of justice. The embodiment of Jewish values, finally empowered to fight anti-Semites and win. My mother took me to Israel when I was 12, and we saw Dayan when we toured the Knesset. She bought me a Star of David necklace, and I have worn one ever since. We were secular Jews and atheists. The star stood for the pride I felt for my people—those who had survived and those who were murdered—and for our traditions of study, of resistance against bigotry, of thoughtful morality, of unflinching intellectual debate.

My mother visited Israel again during the first Gulf War. She declined to don protective headgear when the air raid sirens went off, on the grounds that it would mess up her perm. "They think *these* are bombs!? They don't know what bombardment is!" She strong-armed the husband of a friend into driving her to a West Bank checkpoint, so she could see what all the fuss was about. There she witnessed an Israeli soldier humiliating an elderly Palestinian in front of his grandson. "Maia," she told me on the phone, "it was the Ghetto." My mother had escaped the Warsaw Ghetto days before the liquidation began. Her cousin had been shot in the street for slapping a German soldier who demanded he walk in the gutter.

A few years later, after my mother's memory began to fail, she mailed me the same piece of paper three times, a copy of page 338 of the biography of Theodor Herzl. Underlined is a passage about early Zionist thinker Ahad Ha'am:

"[Ha'am] refused to ignore the presence of Arabs in Palestine.... [In 1889 H]e urged respect for the native population.... 'Yet what do our brethren do in Palestine? Just the opposite. Serfs they were in the lands of the Diaspora. Now, as they suddenly find themselves enjoying unconstrained freedom, they become despots themselves. They treat the Arabs with hostility and cruelty, deprive them of their rights, offend them without cause, and even boast of their deeds....'"

If I had died before my mother, her money would have gone to the Hebrew University of Jerusalem. My mother believed passionately in a homeland for the Jews. Terrorist attacks enraged her. But she despised the infliction of harm upon the vulnerable, and she refused to make an exception for her own people. We never had *the* conversation about Israel, because by the time I began to struggle with my feelings about Israel's occupation of the West Bank and Gaza Strip, such conversations were not possible. She probably never pondered whether Palestinians were inherently anti-Semitic or hated Jews as their oppressors, and she referred to Arabs with the same casual distaste as most Jews her age. But soldiers menacing civilians, with total impunity to act as they please, was something she knew. *Okupacia.*

It was probably harder for me than for her. My mother was a loner, an individualist to her core. Her need to belong had been erased. But I was five when we came to the States, and the warm embrace of the Jewish families who came to our aid gave me safety, a sense of community, a tribe. When I was a teenager, I fantasized about joining the Israeli army. Fighting for my people. Avenging the war.

When I first became aware of opposition to Israel's treatment of Palestinians and Israeli Arabs, I dismissed it as anti-Semitism. Israel, I believed, would do only what was necessary for the survival of the Jewish people. Our values, our experience of oppression, our attachment to justice would permit nothing else. In the early 1980s I read an article in the *Village Voice* describing newly-arrived settlers in the West Bank who had come from Brooklyn. Referring to Arabs as sand niggers, they openly reveled in their new freedom to treat brown-skinned people like they always had wanted to. As enemies and inferiors. I was completely repulsed. And I stored my disgust in a separate compartment of my brain, where it couldn't infect my loyalty to Israel, fighting for survival against hostile neighbors.

It was a photograph—a quarter-page image in the *New York Times* taken in the late 1990s—that finally forced me to integrate new information with the things I wished to believe. In the picture, a clean-shaven young Arab man in a button-down shirt and jeans descends the steps of a government building in Israel. It is May 15th, the day commemorated by some as *Al-Nakbah*, the Catastrophe, when in 1948 large populations of Palestinian people were expelled from the new nation of Israel, their lands turned over to Jews, their villages destroyed. In the photograph, the young man's chin is tucked, he is stumbling, trying to catch his balance, cringing. Behind him four uniformed Israeli soldiers are frozen in the act of pushing him, tearing at his clothes, kicking his legs. And laughing. The contempt in their eyes is unmistakable, as is the fellowship they are feeling. This is what power looks like.

That day I began to know something about Israeli soldiers. Not that they were different from any young men with weapons charged with controlling a civilian population, but that they were the same. That the simple law of occupation operates in the Occupied Territories as it always does: the occupier must dehumanize his subjects, just as his subjects dehumanize him. Occupation breeds rage and resistance, which make the occupier fearful, and in turn more brutal. For years, I had heard American Jews justify Israel's policies by insisting on how much Palestinians hate Jews. Now I understood that were I a Palestinian, I too would hate the Jews. Suddenly I stood apart from the American Jews who appeared on the nightly news to insist on the unimpeachable virtue of the state of Israel.

Since allowing myself to know that Jews, too, are capable of oppression, my opposition to the policies of Israel has roused me to action, but my alienation from the American Jewish mainstream mires me in despair. This was the community that invited me to be American, that reassured me that even if my mother insisted on being a foreigner all her life, I had ties to my new country and would be hailed for the Star of David around my neck. Now, as American perceptions of Israel and Palestine begin tentatively to evolve towards clarity, prominent American Jews embrace censorship and demagoguery, hurling accusations of anti-Semitism at anyone who questions Israel and purging dissenters from Jewish organizations. My people demanded a theatrical performance be closed down because it portrayed Palestinians under occupation as psychically tormented. My people called for a qualified scholar to be denied tenure because she authored a book on the role of archeology in Israel's territorial claims. Faced with the complexity of being held to account despite their own suffering, my people have lost their collective mind. The ecstasy of tribalism has poisoned their hearts.

The simple truth is this: If my mother did not succumb, there's no excuse for anyone. My mother had beloved German friends and hated Germans with a passion. She scorned America for its materialism and intellectual vacuity, and she raised her only daughter in America. My mother accommodated contradictions, not out of a lack of rigor, but out of courage. Out of the ability to see things as they are: complicated, charged, and messy. And demanding of us that we not surrender empathy, even in the face of offense and fear.

The Search for 1948

By Hannah Mermelstein

"Where do you want to go?" asked the taxi driver, expecting to give me a short ride and collect a few shekels.

"Baqa'a," I replied, "but it's a bit of a project."

The West Jerusalem neighborhood of Baqa'a was only a ten-minute drive from our location in East Jerusalem. The "project" was that the house I was looking for had existed 60 years ago, and time travel takes somewhat more detective work than the simple recitation of an address.

"I'm looking for a house from 1948," I told the driver, who introduced himself as Abed. I handed him Munir's diagram of a house that looked similar to hundreds of other old homes in the Jerusalem area.

"Is it yours?" he asked.

"No, a friend's."

I had recently discovered that my friend Munir, whom I know from Boston and had always known as Lebanese, had actually been born in Jerusalem. In 1948, at the age of four, he and his family, along with 800,000 Palestinian people, were forced out of their home by pre-Israeli forces. The family fled to Lebanon, where Munir's father, Najeeb Jirmanus, had lived

19

before moving to Jerusalem 20 years earlier. Nobody in the family had been back to Palestine since 1948, so I asked Munir if, on my next trip to Jerusalem, he would like me to try and find his house. He gathered some information, including a few nearby landmarks and a diagram of the house, which Abed was now studying. Abed agreed to help.

I sat quietly, hoping he knew the neighborhoods well enough to help me. I had planned to seek out an older taxi driver, possibly someone who spoke English so I could make sure to communicate every detail I knew. Abed was a young man who spoke very little English, but he seemed interested in and moved by the project. He immediately began to call all the older people he knew.

"Do you know where the Jordanian embassy was before 1948?" he would ask, offering up our major landmark.

"Yes," one man told him, "but it wasn't in Baqa'a."

"No," said another, "there was barely a Jordan at that time. How could there be a Jordanian embassy?"

So we began to drive, looking for the other smaller landmarks or for people who might recognize Munir's father's name. Abed would pull over next to every older person he saw (Palestinian or Israeli), and ask about the Ummah school, the Jordanian embassy, and the British army women's headquarters. Some people were vaguely helpful, some not. A few informed us in a slightly insulted tone that they were not yet born in 1948.

We left Baqa'a and crossed the street to another, mostly Palestinian neighborhood. We thought we would have a better chance of finding people who wanted to and could actually help, having perhaps been in the neighborhood before 1948. Not two minutes later, we passed an old man and Abed stopped. We got out of the car, said hello, and explained what we were doing.

"You're in luck," said the man, "I know more about these neighborhoods than anyone else in the area."

Before I knew it, his wife was serving me coffee in the middle of the street. The man suggested she and his daughters go ahead without him, as he would join us in the taxi in exchange for a ride home afterwards.

20

We drove for half an hour with little success, and then the man suggested we stop at an old house on the corner. We knocked on the door, and an old Israeli man answered. He took one look at the three of us and asked, "Are you looking for someone who used to live here?" He opened the door and let us in.

"You're in luck," he said, "I know more about these neighborhoods than anyone else in the area."

So here I was inside a house with Abed the taxi driver and two older men, one Palestinian and one Israeli, who said they knew everything there was to know about this part of Jerusalem. They talked for a few minutes and argued amicably for a few more in a combination of Hebrew, Arabic, and English. The interaction had an air of pre-Zionism to it that is difficult to explain. They used language of "Arab" and "Jew" instead of "Palestinian" and "Israeli," which many people do, but it seemed more appropriate in this situation than usual. As though nationalism and the way it has played out could not taint this simple human search for an old home.

I had started the trip late in the day. By this time it was getting dark, and I was running late for a meeting. We had gathered some information that might help us for next time, and I had a few questions to ask Munir. We took our leave, after writing down the name and phone number of the Israeli man so we could try again another day.

* * *

Two weeks later, with semi-clear skies above after a week of nonstop rain, I made plans to meet Abed in Jerusalem. This time, I was armed with more precise directions from Munir, including names of other people who lived and worked in the area and, most importantly, a photograph taken from their front yard in 1940.

Abed met me and excitedly said he knew where the house was, that he had gone back there after our last search. I showed him the photograph and we drove towards the area. We parked and began to walk around, holding up the photograph to each gate and entrance. We found one house that looked similar; however, there was a huge construction project under way directly on top of it. We approached and asked the Palestinian construction workers what they knew about the house, which wasn't much. We were stopped on the way out by an Israeli manager. Abed explained in Hebrew that we were trying to find a house. The man glanced at the photo and said, "Yes, this looks like the house."

Another manager came out and ordered us off the property. "This isn't the house," he said. "There was nothing here before 1948."

Feeling torn, we stood outside for a few minutes and looked around.

"We need to find an Israeli to help us," said Abed finally. "They think you and I are here to claim the house because I'm Arab and you have papers in your hand. They don't know we're only here to look and photograph."

"We should take the house," I replied, only half joking.

At this point, we realized this was probably not the house. The gate looked the same but we couldn't figure out the angles in the photograph and it just didn't seem right. Another older Israeli man on the street asked if he could help. Abed explained that we were searching for a house, and the man joined us for the next 20 minutes as we walked around the neighborhood. We kept finding similar sights, but none of them fit together. Finally he asked, "Are you sure the house is in the German Colony?"

"No," I replied, "it's in Baqa'a."

Apparently, the older Israeli man who had helped us the first time had convinced Abed to come to this area and I, unfamiliar with West Jerusalem's neighborhoods, had gone along for the ride. Realizing we were in the wrong neighborhood, we got back into the car and headed to the Israeli man's house, where we had paused our search two weeks earlier. He answered the door and I shared my new information with him. The house we were searching for was near the Trans-Jordanian consulate, I told him, not the Jordanian embassy, and there was a road that went down from the main street towards their house. These two pieces of information were all he needed. He followed me out to the street, pointed, and said, "Go two more traffic lights. The Allenby building is probably what you mean, and that's on your left. There's a street that goes down from there on the right."

We quickly drove those two blocks, turned right, parked, and started walking down. The streets were different than they were described to me, and the building supposedly on the corner wasn't there. But sure enough, after a few minutes of meandering, I found myself in front of the large building that was in the background of the photo I was holding. I positioned myself exactly at the angle that the photo was taken from, and looked around. One street continued to go down, so I took it. To my right was a synagogue that I guessed was either Munir's property or their neighbor's. I hoped it was not his, that I would not have to tell him his house had been completely destroyed and replaced by a synagogue.

We passed the synagogue and stopped in front of the gate to the next house. This was it. Different from the photo, but with the same dimensions, and seemingly the right distance from the larger building up the street. We entered and found ourselves on the stone path described in the e-mail I had in my hand from Munir's older brother: "...continue along the stone-paved path... some eight meters, you reach the level of the house... Move some 10 more meters and you will have the six stone steps (to the left) that lead up to the veranda and you will then be facing the main door, entrance to the house."

I was facing the main door, the entrance to the house. I thought about knocking on the door, but (in case we didn't get a warm reception here either) wanted to take in as much as possible first. As I walked around the perimeter of the house, I wondered which plants and trees had been there when Munir was a child.

Finally, Abed knocked. No answer. We waited a few minutes and then left. About five minutes later, I came back alone to take more photos, and the door to the house was open.

I walked to the entrance, knocked, and said "hello?" A man appeared.

"My name is Hannah, I'm from the United States, and I have a friend who I think used to live in this house before 1948. Can I come in and look?"

He hesitated, then let me in, introducing himself as Israel. When I asked if I could photograph inside, he hesitated, but again agreed. I asked how long he had been living there, and he replied that it had only been a few years. He said he rented the place from a French Israeli man who has owned it for about five years. Before that, he said, the building was owned by a Moroccan Israeli family.

"Since 1948?" I asked.

"Well, the government probably had it first and then gave it to them, but yes, for a long time."

I kept photographing, staying quiet as I worried he might change his mind. As I was putting my gear away and getting ready to leave, Israel turned to me as though he had something to say.

"The reason I let you in," he said, "is that one time my sister went back to Morocco to find our family house. The man currently living there wouldn't let her in. She cried and cried, and finally he let her in, but he wouldn't let her photograph. This is why I let you in and let you photograph."

Seeing this as an opening, I asked, "Would you want to return to Morocco?"

"No," he replied, almost laughing at the suggestion.

"If the situation changed?"

"No, Morocco is for the Moroccans and Israel is for the Israelis."

"What about the Palestinians?" I replied.

"We were here first," he said, "thousands of years ago. This is our land; it says so in the bible." I had noticed all the Torahs and other religious texts in the house, so it did not surprise me that he was religious.

"Sixty years ago my friend was living here," I said.

"History doesn't start in 1948," he answered.

I briefly considered sharing with him something my Palestinian friend from Hebron often says: "It's written in the Torah that Abraham came here to Hebron and bought a cave, right? Well, who did he buy that cave from? My great, great, great... grandfather!" Knowing, though, that this Israeli man's argument was not rooted in, or concerned with, reliable historic analysis, I decided there was no use arguing with religion. We said an awkward goodbye (saying "thank you" did not seem appropriate in this situation), and I left.

My search for 1948 was almost over. But not quite yet...

* * *

After receiving the photographs I sent, Munir and his brother were thrilled to confirm that this was indeed their house and asked if I might be able to find any legal documentation to corroborate this. Not knowing where to start, I turned to a Canadian-Israeli friend, who agreed to help track down whatever she could. She visited the local Registry of Deeds in Jerusalem, which manages land deeds for the municipality. After being sent from office to office and compiling information about the current address and plot number (according to Israeli zoning laws, not the memories of the prior owners), she finally had the information she needed.

She returned to the Registry of Deeds. The clerk looked at the address and block number and said they had no record of the property before 1992. When she protested, he sent her to the microfilm, saying she could search through it all she wanted. So she did. After almost giving up, she came upon a document that seemed to be for the right property. The document was from the British Mandate period, and was thus written in English. She scanned the paper: 672 square meters, original owners' names... and then, finally, proof of sale of the property in whole on January 6, 1932, to one Najeeb Jirmanus.

* * *

There is something about finding the land registry hidden in the microfilm of Israel's archives (after being told in effect that the property did not exist before 1992) that reminds me that nothing lies too deep under the surface in this part of the world. Beneath every Israeli road lies the dirt of an agricultural path from centuries before. Below every kibbutz field lie the remains of a destroyed Palestinian village. Under all the modern-day addresses and block numbers in the Registry of Deeds office live the memories of a people who cannot forget an old front gate, the very number of steps to their front door, the views from their porch, the place that—despite Israel's refusal to implement the right of return for more than 60 years—many still call home.

Do Not Stand Idly By

By Hedy Epstein

In January 1933, I was an eight-year-old Jewish girl living in the village of Kippenheim, in Germany's Black Forest. That was when Adolph Hitler came to power. Within days, new laws were enacted restricting the rights and freedoms of Jews. I clearly remember Saturday, April 1, 1933, the boycott of all Jewish businesses in Germany. My father and his younger brother ran a business that my great-grandfather had started in 1858. A Nazi stood in front of our store, another in front of the Jewish bakery, the Jewish butcher, the Jewish Hardware store. The boycott not only prevented Christians from shopping in Jewish stores on that day, but it also had long-term effects: Christians were afraid to be seen shopping in Jewish stores, and businesses suffered and closed. Jewish public servants lost their jobs, as did university professors.

Hitler made raving, ranting speeches, which always contained hateful comments about Jews. Soon, books by Jewish writers were publicly burned. The Nazi newspaper *Der Stuermer*, with its terrible caricatures and dreadful stories about Jews, was displayed in glass cases on buildings and kiosks. In September 1935, all German Jews lost their German citizenship. We could no longer go to public swimming pools, sit on benches in public parks, or go to movies, theaters, or concert halls.

As this was happening, my parents tried, with increasing desperation, to leave Germany. I remember my father's repeated plea "*nur raus!*" (just out). They were willing to go anywhere, except one place: Palestine. My parents were secular German Jews. My father proudly fought in World War I. The Jewish families in our village all had little blue metal boxes in their homes in which they collected money to buy trees to be planted in Palestine. We did not have such a box. My parents considered themselves anti-Zionist. The feeling I had then, as well as in retrospect, is that they wanted to live in an integrated society, they were not interested in a country for Jews only.

November 10, 1938, was the last day I went to school in Germany. I attended a private school in a neighboring village about seven kilometers from ours. There was only one other Jewish student, Hans Durlacher, who was in a grade below me.

Shortly after school began, the principal came into our classroom. He talked to all of us, then suddenly stopped, pointed his finger at me, and said: "*Raus mit Dir Du Dreckjude*" (Get out, you dirty Jew.) I thought I must have misunderstood. He was a nice, gentle person, and his daughter was one of my classmates. I asked him to repeat himself. He did, took me by the elbow, and pushed me out of the classroom. As I stood in the hall, thoughts raced through my 14-year-old mind: What did I do? Was I not paying attention? What will I tell my parents?

Before I could answer these questions, the children came out of the classroom, putting on their jackets. Some pushed or shoved me or called me names, and then they all left. Where were they going? I had no idea, so I went back into my classroom, sat at my desk and took out a book. A few minutes later, there was a soft knock on the door, in came Hans. He asked to stay with me. I told him he could stay, but asked him to be quiet so I could study. An hour and a half or so went by. Suddenly, Hans yelled for me to join him at the window. We saw men and boys being marched down the street four in a row, accompanied by Nazi SS storm troopers. The Nazis hit the men and boys with whips, urging them to walk faster. We didn't know the men but assumed they were Jewish. We went to the book store next door to call our parents. I called my mother at home, and a strange voice answered, "the phone is no longer in service." I called my father at his business, then my aunt. Hans called his mother. Each time, we were told "the phone is no longer in service." We each left for home.

When I arrived at my house, I noticed the green shutters were closed. They had been open when I left for school that morning. I ran to the door, and it was locked—I didn't know until that moment that it even could be locked. I rang the doorbell, and no one answered. I stood in front of the building for a few minutes, wondering why nothing made any sense, why everything was different, when I saw a man walking towards me. I knew he was one of the village's worst Nazis. In the past, if I had found myself on the same side of the street as he, I had been so afraid I would cross over to the other side. But that morning, in my dismay, I asked him:

"Do you know where my mother is?"

The man said: "I don't know where the bitch is, but if I find her and she is still alive, I will kill her." Hearing that, I took off as fast as I could. On my way, I passed the Jewish hardware store, its two display windows shattered. Villagers milled about, joking and laughing, and some reached into the broken windows to take merchandise. I didn't understand that either but continued on to my aunt's house. As I got closer, I saw my aunt and mother looking out the window. Then mother opened the door. She looked all wrong, too, tall and thin in my stout, short aunt's baggy, petite dress.

As we stood by the window together, she told me that shortly after I had left for school, some Nazis came to our house and arrested my father. He was wearing his pajamas, and they did not allow him to get dressed nor to put on a coat. A few of the Nazis stayed behind to break our windows, some furniture, and dishes. After they left, my mother closed the shutters, locked the door, and ran to my aunt's house, not realizing she was still wearing her nightgown. My aunt had given her a dress.

They had learned that all Jewish men, and boys 16 and older, had been arrested and taken to village hall. We could see village hall from my aunt's window, and we hoped to see the men released soon. We watched them come out soon after I arrived, but they had not been released. Like the men I'd seen earlier, they were being marched down the street, right past my aunt's house. This time, I recognized many of the men. There was my father in his pajamas, my uncle, many other men and boys I knew. My mother practically hung me out the second-story window, calling to my father:

"We have Hedy, we're together." We didn't know if he heard her or saw me. We watched them march until they went around the bend in the road, and then they disappeared from sight. Where were they going? When would they return? There were no answers, so we closed the window and sat there in numb silence.

Many other things happened that day and night (the infamous Kristallnacht: "the night of broken glass"). Most synagogues were burned to the ground. New laws went into effect: Jewish businesses that had still been open were permanently closed; Jewish doctors and lawyers could no longer practice; Christian doctors were no longer allowed to treat Jews; Jews could not go to hospitals; and Jewish children were no longer allowed to attend either public or private schools.

Because we could not get the windows replaced in our home, we stayed at my aunt's place. I was so traumatized by what I had experienced and seen that day that I did not allow my mother or my aunt out of my sight. If one of us had to go to the bathroom, I insisted that all three of us go together. We all slept in the same bedroom.

We did not know where the men and boys had been taken. We only learned two weeks later, when we received pre-printed postcards from the concentration camp Dachau. It was the first such camp built by the Nazis when they first came to power, although by now there were others. After four weeks, my father returned home an old, broken, sick man.

I don't know what my father endured in the camp. I know now that the men had to sign a statement before being released. If they spoke of what they experienced, they would be returned to Dachau, never to leave again. Also much later, I learned that the reason my father and others were imprisoned was to serve as a lesson for all Jews: if you don't leave Germany, this is what will happen to you.

After my father was relatively well again, he and my mother resumed their efforts to leave Germany. I don't know how or where my parents learned of the Kindertransport, but they understood that if they couldn't get out, they could at least save me. Like almost 10,000 Jewish children who were rescued in the nine months preceding World War II, I was transported to England by train and boat to be placed with a Jewish foster family. I left on May 18, 1939. I was child #5580.

Before I left, my parents spoke brightly of my future on this adventure. They would tell me I'd live in a big city, learn a new language, and attend school again. Always, their last sentence was: "...and we will see each other again soon." I believed that. I don't know if they did. By sending me away, they literally gave me life a second time.

In England, I lived with two foster families, both Jewish. The families were paid to keep me. I started school a few days after my arrival. I stayed with the first one for only two months. They basically starved me while eating regular meals themselves. I was removed from this home and placed with another Jewish family. My parents and I were able to correspond directly with each other and did so regularly until England declared war on Germany on September 3, 1939. The Kindertransports stopped at that time, too.

I still communicated with my parents for another year. We corresponded via 25 word messages through the Red Cross. We also exchanged letters through acquaintances in Switzerland (a neutral country). I stayed with the second family until my 16th birthday, at which time I had to drop out of school and go to work. My first job was as a live-in companion to a 14-year-old girl.

On October 22, 1940, all the Jews from my area of Germany were deported to Camp de Gurs (in Vichy France). There was a long period of no mail from my parents as this occurred. While they were in Camp de Gurs, we were able to correspond directly with each other. They were allowed to write only one page per person per week; I could write as often and as much as I wanted to.

In an August 9, 1942 letter, my father wrote: "tomorrow I am being deported to an unknown destination, and it may be a long time before you hear from me again."

In a September 1, 1942 letter, my mother wrote the same. I received a final postcard from her, dated September 4, 1942, which reads: "Traveling to the East... sending you a final goodbye." My parents both perished at Auschwitz in 1942. It took me years to accept that we would not be together again.

I belonged to a German, mostly Jewish political organization in London, Free German Youth, whose major objective was to return to Germany after World War II and teach Germans democratic principles. After the war's end in 1945, I saw a sign on a building inviting people to inquire about doing interesting work in Germany. The job would be my ticket to Germany. After filling out forms and passing tests, I was ready to go to work for the US Civil Censorship Division. My job was to censor incoming and outgoing German mail for possible coded messages (I never found any). I was not yet 21, so I needed my parents' or guardians' permission to take the position. Since I had neither, I pleaded and begged, and was ultimately allowed to go.

When the train stopped the first time in Germany, young children on the platform stood begging for candy and cookies. Some of the people on the train, refugees just like me, gave the children whatever they had. I became very angry, saying:

"How can you give something to these Nazis?" Some of these kids were five or six; they weren't Nazis, of course. I became aware at that very moment how full of hatred I was of Germans, even little children. My plan was to stay in Germany and work for democracy, but I realized that would be impossible to do if I hated everyone.

Before my one year contract was up, I decided to stay in Germany a while longer but wanted to find more interesting work. I learned that the US component at the Nuremberg International Trial of the Nazi "elite" needed workers. I was hired as a research analyst assigned to the trial of Nazi doctors who had performed medical experiments on concentration camp inmates. My job was to look for the documentary evidence to be used by the prosecution. I was not prepared for what I found in the documents. I often was sick to my stomach and had nightmares (in fact, on occasion still have nightmares even now about these experiments). It was not only the written words, describing in detail the gruesome minutia of the experiments and the victims' reactions, but photographs sometimes accompanied the descriptions.

When I sat in on the trial, a young female survivor testified about the experiments conducted by one of the defendants, Herta Oberhaeuser. Asked if she could identify the person who operated on her, she pointed to Oberhaeuser, whose facial expression and body language showed no feeling. Oberhaeuser was later asked why she performed these particular experiments. Her response: "They were just Polish women who were going to die anyway."

I have always wondered what the world has learned and applies from the precedents set at Nuremberg. The world is a slow learner.

After the trials, my hatred of Germans still seething, I knew I had to leave. I did not wish to return to England. At the invitation of my only surviving relatives—my mother's younger brother and his wife—I immigrated to the United States in May 1948, at about the same time Israel became a state.

I had mixed feelings about Israel. On one hand, I was glad that there was a place for Holocaust survivors who either could not or chose not to return to their country of origin. On the other hand, remembering my parents' anti-Zionism, I feared no good would come of it. But I was new in the US, with so much to learn and do, so Israel/Palestine was on the back burner of my interest and remained there for a long time.

After all my time alone, my aunt and uncle's love for me was overwhelming. I was no longer used to such abundant love. As soon as I could, I moved out of their home and into a furnished room not too far from them. I took a job at the New York Association for New Americans, an agency bringing over primarily Jewish displaced persons who survived the Holocaust. I worked in the shelter where these survivors were housed until they were re-located throughout the US I realized much later that taking this job had been no coincidence. It was a subtle way to search for my parents or someone who knew something about them.

I also became involved in American politics: Henry Wallace's presidential campaign; civil rights; the Ethel and Julius Rosenberg case.

My job ended, and in 1950 I moved to St. Paul/Minneapolis, Minnesota, working for some years for the Jewish Family & Children's

Service. I helped displaced persons file their restitution claims against the German government for personal and material losses under the Nazi regime. Once again, I understand in looking back, I was hoping to find my parents or news about them among the clients. Politically, I became involved specifically in housing discrimination against African Americans. In 1953, after five years in the country, I applied for US citizenship. This was during the McCarthy era, and I was interrogated and investigated for almost six years because (I believe) of my association with the Free German Youth. In the meantime, I got married and had my son, Howard, in 1956. I enjoyed being a wife and mother. It was the first time since I had turned 16 that I did not work for a living. My second pregnancy shattered my new, idyllic life. After complications, my baby was born prematurely and died due to underdeveloped lungs.

I was devastated by the loss of the baby. I believe my husband felt relieved—he'd been waiting to move the family to St. Louis for his job, and had been impatient and angry at the pregnancy-related delays. This was the beginning of the parting of our ways. In 1960, I became a US citizen. In 1961, we moved to St. Louis. I was still grieving, grieving for a long time. I went through my days mechanically, performing my motherly and housewifely tasks as needed, feeling ever more removed from my husband (we did not divorce until 1974). In the spring of 1963, I started to do some volunteer work. Some time in 1964, a friend took me to a board meeting of the Greater St. Louis Committee for Freedom of Residence (a nonprofit fair housing agency). I volunteered, then worked for the committee and became its director.

In the meantime, the Viet Nam War was raging. In the spring of 1970, it became public knowledge for the first time that as part of this awful war, we had been carpet-bombing Cambodia for several months prior. This information spurred me to renewed action. I picketed, marched, and sent letters to politicians. It was in doing so that I finally got over my hatred of Germans. Writing and sending these letters, I realized that I was free to do so with no fear of reprisal for me or my family. If, during World War II, German individuals had done what I was now doing, they would have been sent to a concentration camp and likely lost their lives.

I realized then that I could not condemn an entire people for not being willing to risk their lives, when I didn't know that I would be willing to risk mine. With that realization, the hatred dissipated. I have been back to Germany many times, especially since 1995 (after I retired) for speaking engagements. While I have no home in Germany anymore, I feel at home there. A few years ago, I applied for and regained the German citizenship taken from me in 1935.

I was aware of the 1967 and 1973 Israeli wars but, other than being opposed to war, was not involved. It was not until 1982 that Israel/Palestine returned to the forefront of my mind. I heard about the Sabra and Shatila massacre in a meeting of a mainstream Jewish community group. This massacre of Palestinian and Lebanese refugees was committed by Christian militia—but the camps were surrounded and controlled by the Israeli military that let the militia in. The community group's reaction shocked me—they applauded. I could feel my hair standing up on end. Why were Jews supporting a massacre?

I felt the need to know what this was all about. I began to educate myself about what happened between 1948 and 1982, when I paid little attention to this part of the world. As I learned and understood more, I became increasingly distraught, then horrified, by the policies and practices of the Israeli government and military toward the Palestinians. I began to publicly state my opposition.

In 2001, I started the St. Louis chapter of Women in Black. Since then, we have continued to hold vigils once a month in opposition to Israel's occupation of Palestinian land and people. During a vigil against the Iraq war in September 2003, my dear friend Dianne turned to me and asked, "Have you ever thought about going to Palestine?" I hadn't, but spontaneously said "yes."

So, Dianne, two other women, and I arrived in the West Bank in December 2003. The very first non-violent demonstration I participated in, together with other internationals, Israelis, and Palestinians, was in opposition to the gate in the "security fence" in Mas'ha, which had not been opened for two weeks, keeping farmers from their fields. As we neared the gate, Israeli soldiers shot at us with live ammunition. The very first person critically injured (his aorta was severed, but he survived) was a young Israeli. Just two weeks prior, he had been released from his three-year mandatory military service.

During this visit, I stayed with a Palestinian family in Ramallah. A year earlier, their then 11-year-old son had been playing in his front yard when he was attacked and beaten by several Israeli soldiers. He was so traumatized that he could not yet sleep in his own bed a year later. He was afraid to leave the house alone and would not play outside. His parents had to take him to school and pick him up, because he was afraid to go alone or even in the company of his schoolmates.

When Dianne and I were leaving to come home from that first trip, I was stopped by Israeli security at the airport. I was 79 at the time. I do not know if they knew I was a survivor (though my passport states that I was born in Germany), but they knew where I had been and what I had been doing. After being frisked, I was asked to get undressed. I asked the 20-something woman why and told her I wanted an attorney. These were her words: "Because you are a terrorist, because you are a security risk. Yes, you can have an attorney, but until you get one, you will be detained at the airport detention center."

I did not know where Dianne was or what was happening to her, so I submitted, thinking, maybe if I do, I will get out, and I can help her if necessary. Besides, I had no attorney, and they'd taken my cell phone, how would I go about getting one? After I was undressed, the woman asked me to bend over.

"Why?" I asked again.

"Because I need to examine you internally," she said.

I demanded she change her gloves, which she'd been wearing since she began the process, but she replied:

"They are clean."

"No, they are not clean," I told her. "You patted me down with them on, and my clothes are not clean."

After a few more minutes of argument, she finally took off her gloves, threw them in a corner, and put on new ones. She then performed a cavity search, both vaginally and rectally. Finally, I was allowed to get dressed and come out of the cubicle we'd been standing in and into the larger airport police area. Other airport security people were meticulously searching through my luggage. Three hours into this ordeal, Dianne was brought into the room and was very surprised to see me. She thought I was already aboard the plane. They went through her belongings the same way.

"Everything has already been checked," Dianne said, as furious as I. "Don't you trust your people downstairs?" They ignored her and kept working. We were detained for a total of five hours. We were re-booked on an El Al flight leaving the following morning and told we could leave the airport and return the next day.

"We're not going through this again tomorrow," I said. "We're going to stay at the airport." We were escorted to departures, where we spent a long, sleepless night. The next morning, we boarded the plane. My anger needed an outlet, and I didn't have much of one seated on that airplane. I took all the magazines out of the seat pocket in front of me (and in front of Dianne). On each page of each magazine, I wrote, sometimes pressing so hard I tore the pages:

"I am a Holocaust survivor. I will never, ever return to Israel."

Obviously, I did not adhere to that pledge, because just five months later, I was back in the West Bank. After returning home, I received some counseling, which helped to constructively channel my anger. I also wrote an article that appeared in the February 17, 2004, *St. Louis Post Dispatch*. In it I stated, " ...but I refuse to be terrified by... such unnecessary disrespect. It is a cruel illusion that force of this sort provides security to Israel... Similarly, humiliating Palestinians cannot extinguish their hopes for a homeland...," and so I have been back to the West Bank four more times since 2003.

Several years ago in the West Bank, I met, traveled and protested with two women who are among the founders of the Free Gaza Movement (FGM). When they asked me to become part of FGM and travel to Gaza, my instant response was: "Yes, of course." In fact, I felt honored to be asked. FGM's goal is to break the siege of this tiny 25- by 6- mile territory with a population of 1.5 million people. Walled in and cut off from the world, Gaza is the largest open-air prison in the world.

I was to be on one of the two boats that traveled to Gaza in August 2008. In preparation, I took swimming lessons at age 83. I was excited to be part of this historic event and to stand in solidarity with the Gazan people. Waiting in the heat of Larnaca, Cyprus, for several hot, humid days, I got a terrible headache and fainted. Though I felt this was a minor event, the group became very concerned. With great regret but in deference to them, I did not go. I was scheduled to go to Gaza again on FGM's June 2009 boat trip to Gaza. On the day before I was to leave home, I was assaulted. The injuries I sustained prevented me from my second attempt to go to Gaza. This boat, a tiny unarmed vessel containing only humanitarian aid, was seized (illegally—pirated, in other words) by the Israeli military. Its unarmed passengers, including a former US congresswoman and a Nobel Prize winner, were put in Israeli jails and deported.

Whenever it happens, I plan to be on the next voyage. By traveling to Gaza, I hope to fulfill one of Judaism's most basic values, as stated in Leviticus 19:16: "Do not stand idly by when your neighbor's blood is shed." I can not stand idly by when people are dying from starvation, disease, and lack of medical care, and while they lack adequate housing, access to education, and freedom to travel.

I do not like to make comparisons (though I'm sometimes accused of doing that) between Germany and Israel. Here, I am just telling the truth: When I stood for the first time next to the 25-foot-high cement wall in Qualqulia, the motto of Holocaust survivors came unbidden to me: "Never again." Sadly, I wondered when its meaning had become, "Never again for the Jews, now by them." That is not the lesson of the Holocaust, not for me. To me, "never again" means never to anyone, and it also means that it is my duty, as long as I am able to do it, to "not stand idly by" as others suffer.

It is the responsibility of each of us to give voice to those who have been forgotten and forsaken by a seemingly uncaring world. I strongly believe that ordinary citizen activism can be a force for peace. It is the best reason I know to do what I have been doing, to go to where the silence is and then report back what I have seen and experienced on the ground. The Israeli government's arrogance, its *chutzpah*, and its violent practices stand in the way of accomplishing the peace Israelis say they want. It stands in the way of Palestinians having the same rights all human beings deserve.

The Palestinians will not go away. They are a resilient, ever-hopeful people. They are my sisters and brothers.

Abandoned Palestinian houses and shops forcibly evacuated in order to create a physical security barrier for the protection of Jewish residents in the area. (Hebron)

Although Palestinian residents are not allowed back to their old shops or houses, Jewish residents are free to move about there and often vandalize and steal. (Hebron)

My Feet Were Praying

By Sandra Butler

Previously published in 2007 in Turning Wheel, *an American Buddhist publication.*

In all my years of political activism, I never broke the taboo against criticizing my own people, my Jewish family. Yet my religious studies and the news of an increasingly draconian set of limitations on Palestinian life left me feeling tentative and uncertain. I have been armed to the teeth with both left and feminist analysis most of my political life. Which side are you on, the labor union song asks? I always thought I knew what side I was on and who was on it with me. I thought those on the other side were misguided or ignorant. So how do I condemn my own Jewish family?

My assessment of the imposed suffering of the Palestinian people, inevitably leading to the moral atrophy of the Jewish state, leaves me feeling alienated from those I love, casting me out onto the margins of the Jewish world. My grandmother would say that just because I am becoming increasingly knowledgeable about ancient Jewish texts does not mean that I have the right to speak against my own people. My mother would echo her, accusing me of betraying Jews who have been oppressed, she sighs, since forever. Sticking my nose where it doesn't belong, my father might add. Yet perhaps my grandfather would have been the one to understand. He is the one who taught me about injustice, educated me about poor and oppressed people, about the dignity of every person, and always, he added sternly, no matter who. I want to believe he would understand that most of the poor and oppressed people in Israel/Palestine are Palestinians living in refugee camps, and that I am acting in the name of his teachings.

To add insult to the internal dissonance, many American Jews condemn me as a self-hating Jew, and secular left-wing activists with whom I often find common cause incorporate anti-Semitic language and interpretations into their rhetoric against me, blurring the Israeli army and government with the Israeli people, and even more virulently, with Jews around the world.

Now I am 67 years old, all my ancestors are dead, and I am left behind to hear my own voice, to make my way through the underbrush of contradictions and sense of disloyalty, yet with an urgency to face squarely and unapologetically the Israeli re-enactment of our own oppressive history, now directed against the Palestinian people.

All my life, I created stories to help me make sense of the world. I created the stories, then I believed in them. Inevitably, as life intervened, the stories dissolved, leaving me with more complex and often painful realities. My central story about Israel was based on the belief that there were parallel narratives, an equivalently urgent Israeli and Palestinian history, that there were real dangers Israel had to protect against. I was carefully taught that the state of Israel was a refuge for persecuted and tormented remnants of a vibrant and rich world of European Jews after World War Two. I saw that singular truth, and no other.

In these past years, I have immersed myself in this region of the world, its convoluted history and geography, and struggled over pages in hundreds of books, each of which defined what it meant to be a good Jew, to create *tikkun olam*, mending, repairing, and restoring our broken world. As I studied, I deepened my prayer practice, reciting the central daily prayer of the Jewish faith tradition.

Sh'ma Israel. Adonai Eloheinu. Adonai Echod. (Hear O Israel. The Lord Our God the Lord is One.)

Judaism affirms, through the repetition of the Sh'ma, the oneness of all life, all beings, and the earth itself. There is no duality between mind and body, between earth and person. It is all Echod One. Feminist scholar Judith Plaskow urges us to glimpse the One in and through the changing forms of the many, to see the whole in and through its infinite images. Despite the fractured, scattered, and conflicted nature of our experience, there is a unity that embraces and contains our diversity and that connects all things to each other.

Women hold an anti-occupation peace vigil in Israel

Now, as I listen and struggle to remember my dedication to the oneness of all things, I push against criticism, shame, as well as the sense of moral disappointment and personal outrage at the draconian oppression Israelis are carrying out against Palestinian people. How do I keep from arming myself with anger and judgment, separating myself from the Israeli government's actions and all its supporters? How do I ask my broken heart to stay open? How do I express my oppositional truth with fierce love?—like my grandfather taught me, no matter who or what!

Challenged by members of his conservative congregation about why he chose to march with Martin Luther King in Selma, Alabama, in 1965,

Rabbi Abraham Joshua Heschel responded, "My feet were praying." For me, standing in the street with Women in Black is my public expression of the Amidah, our daily prayer.

I just returned from several weeks in Israel/Palestine, where I attended the 13th International Women in Black Conference on Resisting War and Occupation. We gathered, more than 700 strong, to vigil, to teach and study together, to extract from our many struggles in countries around the world, the lessons of peace-making and non-violent struggle against all forms of militarism and nationalism. While my trip provided only a snapshot of the constantly changing realities that both Israelis and Palestinians face, my eyes and my heart fill with an altered reality, requiring me to dismantle my remaining protective stories and see clearly what is.

What I saw was a series of concrete barriers separating people from land, past from future, a blank impassive wall straddling two worlds, the wounds of people echoing and magnifying one another. I saw violence done to the soil and to the people, as the knifepoint edge of the ubiquitous bulldozer slices through land that has been at rest for centuries, carving up the ancestors and their memories. I saw Israeli soldiers guarding one small Israeli house on a naked hillside surrounded by Palestinian villages, in preparation for the expansion of Israeli settlements. I saw a concrete wall that divided a main street in a Palestinian village in half so that Israeli traffic could run more smoothly. I heard an Israeli, who when asked to move his car from the center of a narrow street in a Palestinian neighborhood in the Old City, reply contemptuously, "Why should I move my car? It's my street."

I saw Palestinian men and women walking along a dirt path to a checkpoint, vulnerable to the whims of the young Israeli soldiers on duty. I smelled the tear gas thrown at Palestinian villagers at the end of a demonstration after the internationals had returned to the safety of their buses. I watched the smiling face of the young Palestinian woman, whose house was to be demolished that week, offer us sugar pita bread to thank us for caring about her life and the future of her neighbors. I saw the fury on the face of an Israeli settler as Israeli, Palestinian and international demonstrators held vigils at the entrance to the settlement of Ariel, his face clenched as he slammed on his brakes and flew out of the car to snatch the Palestinian flag from the hands of a local Palestinian activist proudly holding it. I watched as several police officers tried to subdue him.

And repeatedly, I saw the steady determined faces of villagers, activists, and internationals, many of whom have lived through two periods of *intifada*, the Palestinian protests against the Israeli occupation of the West Bank, Gaza and East Jerusalem. These are the women and men who are living their politics day after day, with heartbreaking losses and occasional small successes.

At the Conference, there were visible and invisible walls with the potential to divide women from one another—those who wanted to engage in demonstrations and those with concerns for personal safety. There were women whose focus was on issues relevant to the Israel/Palestine struggle, and women from all over the world with wide-ranging concerns. There were secular and religious Jews, conservative and radical Palestinians. Women who insisted upon lesbian visibility, and those who wanted to honor and respect the slowly changing conservative Palestinian cultural norms. Complexity and paradox all scrambled together. Yet in Jerusalem, a city of so many overlapping loyalties and priorities, the walls dividing us fell as we sat in overcrowded small rooms and began to speak. Everyone was heard; each woman's perspective was respected and given space. There was no cross talk, there were no arguments, interruptions, criticism. Each conversation was intricate, touching deep chords in women's histories and lives. There was great freedom in the way we listened, in the respect for multiple locations and ideas, patience with inexperience and delight in welcoming newcomers to international concerns. I stretched for the best in myself as I sat in circle after circle of women—from the former Yugoslavia, Italy, Britain, Palestine, Israel, Columbia, Guatemala and the US—and together we found our way through the thickets of identity, solidarity, nationalisms and feminist theory. We felt our way forward into the future of justice and of peace. As I listened, my breathing grew deeper, slower, and more spacious.

And, as women joined Palestinian, Israeli and international activists to sing songs of liberation in Bi'lin, a besieged Palestinian village whose land is being remorselessly confiscated for the expansion of the adjoining settlement, my feet were praying. We stood in silence before the concrete wall that bisects history and geography, facing the armed and jittery Israeli soldiers, our voices rising into the air over the rooftops of homes about to be demolished. Beside us stood the children of the village, smiling, making peace signs and asking us their only English phrase, "What is your name?"

My feet were praying when we stood, hundreds strong, lining both sides of the Kalandia checkpoint as thousands of Palestinians moved between us, necessary papers in hand. Some met our eyes and nodded, others simply moved through the familiar dusty corridor of fence-lined passage.

My feet were praying when I joined international activists at the entrance to an Israeli settlement, joined by a local Palestinian woman, proudly holding her national flag, nearly enveloped by Israeli soldiers and a cluster of armored vehicles there to protect us from the settlers. We stood in the fierce noon-time sun, eyes straight ahead as the cars streamed past us, drivers and passengers cursing, waving their fists, children peering out through the back window, looking bewildered.

In Palestine, standing before a demolished house, a carcass of concrete and rubble, I recited the *Kaddish*, the Jewish prayer for the dead.

I am growing lighter. As I approach the end of my 60s, I am finding the courage to release the heavy wrappings of my defenses. I feel the winds of possibility on my skin now, as unprotected as my heart. It has taken my whole life to reach this place.

Up Against The Wall

By Susan Greene

"The globe shrinks for those who own it; for the displaced or the dispossessed, the migrant or the refugee, no distance is more awesome than the few feet across borders or frontiers."
—Homi Bhabha

For close to a year, Maisa, Assia, Ishak, Nidal, and Shaad Aamer have looked out their front door and instead of seeing their garden, animal shed and beyond to their village, they are confronted by an enormous, gray, concrete wall. In the village of Mas'ha, West Bank, Palestine, the children of Hani Aamer live surrounded on all four sides by the Apartheid Wall or Separation Fence, depending on one's perspective. Although the wall running through Mas'ha is actually a fence topped with barbed wire, in November 2003, the Israeli army erected a concrete section, twenty-four feet high and one hundred twenty feet long, directly in front of the Aamer home. This was the Israeli response when the family refused to accept a blank check to move from their land. An Israeli settlement comes right up to the back of the property, a mere twenty feet away.

The Aamer home sits between the two main gates into the village. Family members are forced to let themselves and others in and out through a locked gate, which sends an alarm to the Israeli army every time it is opened. For nearly a year, the Aamers did not have their own key to the gate, nor were they allowed visitors. The family was threatened with home demolition if they violated the order. After their situation was publicized on Israeli television, the army commander agreed to let the Aamers have a key to the gate and, with prior Israeli army approval, periodic visits from family members.

I met the Aamer family on July 18, 2004. Sponsored by the International Women's Peace Service (IWPS), my partner Eric Drooker and I arrived in Mas'ha as volunteers for Break the Silence Mural Project. We were very curious to meet this family and planned to ask if they would be interested in painting a mural on the wall that cut through their land. To this first meeting, we brought art supplies and conducted a drawing project with about fifteen neighborhood youngsters while their parents looked on. We asked the children to draw pictures of their hopes for the future and then asked the parents what they thought about a mural. "Yes!" was the instant response of Munira, the mother of the family, and Hani, the father, also immediately agreed. They told their excited children that we would soon return to paint with them.

A few days later, Eric and I—joined by IWPS and members of two Israeli organizations, Anarchists Against the Wall and Black Laundry— met at the gates to the Aamer house and stopped at the red sign that threatened: "Warning: Mortal Danger for Damaging the Fence." Israeli soldiers and settlement police arrived quickly and questioned us all.

"Are you going to paint on the wall?"

"No, we are doing an art project with the children, but, you know how children are..."

The soldiers collected all our passports, said they must obtain permission for our visit, and noted that because our group included Jewish Israeli citizens, they had a particular obligation to protect our safety. They retreated to their jeeps, and when they were a safe distance away, we discussed the irony that at this exact spot just months earlier, Israeli soldiers had shot an unarmed Jewish Israeli protester with live ammunition. Twenty agonizing minutes later, the soldiers returned the passports, and the Aamer family was allowed to open the gate.

The children ran up to us, shaking our hands and saying hello. They asked in English: "How are you?" and "What's your name?" Tea was served, and Eric and I started mixing bright colors. Without any prompting, and despite the army Jeep sitting outside the fence twenty yards away, the children joyfully and vigorously started painting on the wall—fish, a large bird with a snake in its mouth, hills, flowers, several bright yellow suns, trees, faces, and many, many houses. Eric painted a phoenix in flight. More than twenty children painted with us. Then their parents and neighbors joined in. Eric and I somewhat nervously watched the Israeli army as they watched us the whole time. At one point, a Jewish Israeli settler stood outside the gate conversing with the soldiers and watching, then finally left. We worried that at any moment they would stop us. We were putting a lot of paint on the wall. At about two p.m., Hani Aamer came back from his fields with his cart and donkey. To get into the enclosure, he had to open the larger gate, to which he had no key. We watched as the soldiers opened the gate for Hani to enter his property. Hani's kids ran up and jumped on the cart for a ride. Soon after, the Israeli soldiers came in and told us they wanted us to leave immediately.

We packed up our paint and went inside the house for one more cup of tea.

Now, when they looked out the front door, the Aamer family would see a yellow and orange phoenix rising up from an almost psychedelic green valley dotted with red flowers, brilliant suns, large animals and houses. Of course, the wall was still there. The IDF and settlement were still there. But the view from the front door of the Aamer family home had begun to change, recording the family's engagement in a collaborative public act of creative resistance and solidarity.

A week after the painting party, I returned to the Aamer family to interview them. I had a research grant from the Palestinian American Research Center to analyze what public art projects such as this one mean to all the participants. Would it be possible to determine the effects of the project? What did solidarity mean in this context? The mission of Break the Silence Mural Project includes using culture to bring back stories of Palestine to an American audience. What did the project say about the Aamers' life? What did it mean to the family to work with Jewish Americans and Jewish Israelis? What did it mean for me, a Jewish American, to collaborate on public art projects with Palestinians?

Munira Aamer said, "The wall continues to be a wall, but the mural has made it easier for us to look at it. The mural creates some pleasure and relief for me and my children. The mural changed the view—now I am looking at something alive, and before I saw it as the end of the world, a disaster. Now when I look at it, I see birds, suns, and flowers. This view is beautiful and good. Before it was only scary. My children are very happy and proud of their painting in the mural. My kids see life when they see the mural. The mural was like opening a window for the world. One day the wall will be demolished. I wish I could open this cage and fly with my children, like the free bird in the mural."

Hani Aamer said, "When the Israeli government started building the wall, many people from all over the world came to support our resistance to it. The government arrested or took all of the supporters and deported them. The Israelis told me that the people who came to help me were no longer here. They said: 'You are now alone. Who is going to help you?' But the solidarity people, including Israeli solidarity people, came back to help us again. It lifted my spirits when the solidarity people came back to paint on the wall. My kids started to play outside again. For a year, they were so sad they would not play outside. When you come to paint with the children, it makes them feel like they can live."

Munira Aamer continued, "The children remember who painted with them on the wall, and they remember the experience of painting with their friends. When we look at the wall, we remember who painted each section and how it felt to paint together."

The family asked when we would return to finish the mural. The painting had only gone up to where a six-foot ladder allowed. Two-thirds of the wall was still unpainted concrete, in stark contrast to the colors of the mural at the bottom.

"People who come by want to know why the painters didn't finish. They say the mural should cover the whole wall," Munira said. "The people who came and worked with us value the ideas of the mural—that is good and we hope that they will cover more of the wall."

* * *

And so the next summer, 2005, we returned to the Aamer home to finish the mural. Together with the family and their friends, a group of young Palestinian women activists called Flowers Against the Occupation, members of the IWPS, and Anarchists Against the Wall, we prepared to paint the sky. The first day, the painting continued until about two p.m., when the Israeli soldiers intervened. They invaded the yard barking orders and asserted their power with sub-machine guns. We tried to argue with them, as did some neighbors of the Aamer family, to no avail. There was a palpable sense of, anger, frustration, and resignation among the Palestinians. A neighbor, standing on the porch in close proximity to several Israeli soldiers, angrily threw down her cup of tea. Several of the men present whisked her away, and then negotiated frantically with the Israeli soldiers, who decided to let it go.

It was unclear whether we would be permitted access the following day, but a different crew of soldiers was at the gate and they were polite, stopped us for a while, and then permitted us to enter. They seemed unaware of the previous day's events. Children poured into the area joyously, many more than the day before, as word had spread that the American painters were back. We continued to paint the sky while drinking many rounds of tea.

At around two p.m., Hani Aamer phoned to say the painting had to stop immediately. We had no idea why, but knew that if Hani said we had to go, it must be serious. Later, we learned that because of the "disengagement" of settlers from Gaza taking place at that moment, the Israeli army perceived the mural painting as a provocation to the nearby Jewish settlement. The IDF had threatened Hani with taking back the family's key to the gate if we did not leave immediately.

Hani Aamer later explained his dilemma. "The soldier is telling me that the visitors should leave. They are my visitors who come to support me and stand in solidarity with us and I cannot tell them to leave. They come from England and the United States. They are guests in my house. I cannot throw them out." Yet Hani Aamer had to do just that. This act of the Israeli army commander forcing Hani to ask his visitors to leave, instead of ordering us to do so himself, was an infliction of additional pain. For Hani, treating guests in a rude or inhospitable way was completely unacceptable and humiliating, especially guests who had come from so far.

A view of a portion of the concrete apartheid wall

We packed up our materials, leaving the leftover paint and brushes behind for the Aamer family. After a final defiant cup of tea, we left the premises. We had planned a mural opening the following day, but since the mural was not completed, we held a press conference instead. Very few reporters showed up, in part because everyone was focused on the forced removal of the settlers from Gaza. We took advantage of the time and opportunity to interview Hani. Someone suddenly appeared and urged me to follow quickly.

I ran back to the gate, and Munira let me in. This was the first time I had been on the Aamer property without a large group present. I had an immediate and shocking sense of what life was like for this family. It was eerily quiet, and sounds echoed off the concrete wall. I now understood much more clearly how cut off the Aamers really were from the village of Mas'ha and their community. They had been relegated to a bizarre existence in which they were much closer to and in full view of an illegal Israeli settlement. The settlement's inhabitants were armed and often directed violence at the family, such as breaking windows and destroying the chicken coop. Munira and I went inside her home, and I saw that she had not, despite Israeli military orders, stopped painting the day before. Beginning with the sky blue from the mural, she had begun to paint the rooms of her house. She had started with a bedroom and painted the ceiling and walls. The morning light streamed in and the room was glowing. As I stood in the living room, I could see both blues, of the mural and of the bedroom, from my peripheral vision. The project of solidarity, resilience, and resistance had moved from outside to inside the house. Munira Aamer had refused to stop painting and she was very pleased with her efforts.

* * *

In subsequent conversations with the family, I heard that slowly—room by room—Munira continued painting, using up all the mural paint that did not make it to the wall outside. One of her daughters wants to go to art school, and people in the US have been holding benefits to help make that dream a reality.

Break the Silence is funded in part by the generous support of the Middle East Children's Alliance and the Palestine American Research Center.

Only 30 Miles
But a World Away

By Tomi Laine Clark

It took me five buses and four hours to get roughly 30 miles from Tel Aviv to the Jalazun refugee camp north of Ramallah. The first leg involved taking an *Egged* bus from the central train station in Tel Aviv to Jerusalem. From the main bus station in Jerusalem, I took another bus to Jaffa Gate, just outside of the Old City. I knew I had to get to the Arab bus station near Damascus Gate, which I discovered was about halfway around the wall of the Old City.

I walked, and as I did I noticed the passersby slowly begin to change form. In only a few minutes they were no longer short and t-shirt clad tourists or *kippah*-wearing Torah readers. They were women in long coats and scarves, pulling children along in the sweltering heat. They were dark-skinned men in polo shirts and leather sandals yelling boisterously at each other from across the street. They were sellers of trinkets and refreshments whose wares were simply stacked on the sidewalk and available for one or two shekels. Upon reaching Damascus Gate, I asked some men how to get on a bus to Ramallah. They responded with the utmost courtesy, giving me directions in excellent English and in great detail, down to how many meters I should walk.

The bus station in East Jerusalem was markedly different from its counterparts in both Tel Aviv and West Jerusalem. There was trash everywhere, no shade, and certainly no air-conditioned waiting area. Absent, too, was the neatly ordered queue I was used to. Here, I flagged down the bus as it exited the station. It slowed to a crawl but did not stop. I grabbed the door, jumped on, and attempted to ask how much the fare was but was waved away as the bus lurched forward out of the station.

We were not stopped at the *machsom*, or checkpoint, when we entered the West Bank, but I noticed a sign as we passed through that said, in Hebrew, "No Israelis Allowed." The scenery abruptly changed. The ubiquitous monolith known as "the security barrier" was still there, but now it was covered with graffiti for a "Free Palestine." Also visible was "Zionism is Racism" and "I am not a terrorist." Short but powerful was the 20-meter-wide "CTRL + ALT + DELETE." Rubble was everywhere, as was barbed wire, garbage, and a scattered group of the downtrodden. They were trying to sell things to their fellow Palestinians.

My first trip through a *machsom* coincided almost exactly with my second wedding anniversary. This was not my first trip to Israel, but it was the first time I had ventured across the border into the West Bank.

In July, two years earlier, I married an Israeli, and we visited his homeland the following spring. It was not only my first time in Israel, but my first time out of my own country. I grew up in the Midwest with my single mother and no siblings. It was just the two of us most of the time, and we moved around a lot, so I never learned to make friends easily. My husband Carmel, however, has always been a social butterfly. He loves meeting new people so much that he would sometimes invite strangers home after striking up a conversation with them on the street. At first, I was appalled and offended when, standing at the stove stirring a pot, I was presented with a pair of sheepish strangers. Explanation was seldom offered. Soon I stopped asking him to at least warn me. And then, wonder of wonders, there came a day when he brought no strangers home with him, and I felt... disappointed. This was the beginning of my "Israelization." Carmel had unwittingly prepared me for immersion in Israel just by being unfailingly, maddeningly, and lovably Israeli.

When I arrived in Tel Aviv, I was sufficiently prepared to greet my in-laws with hugs and kisses instead of handshakes but still not prepared for the endless parade of guests through my mother-in-law's home. Bilha was just as social as Carmel but had a 30-year head start on friend accumulation. Everyone wanted to lay eyes on Carmel's new wife. Their questions were endless, invasive and, regrettably, in almost-perfect English. I could not claim I didn't understand them. They wanted to know what I did for a living, how much money I made, how much college I had completed. They were obsessively attentive. At times, I simply had to excuse myself and sit alone in the bedroom for a few minutes.

Later, I would find that attentiveness one of those most endearing aspects of Israeli culture, because it also presents itself in much more pleasing ways. For example, if I was served tea and sugar but no spoon, all I had to do was raise my eyes to the table in front of me and my host would present a spoon to answer my searching glance. If I had come in from a hot day, I was offered a shower. If I yawned, I was offered a quiet room in which to take a nap. Just as in any culture, you take the good with the bad. Characteristic of her gregarious, unapologetic sense of humor, Bilha told me a joke that went, "Why don't Israelis have sex in cars? Because everyone who drives by will stop and tell you how to do it."

I found my in-laws warm and welcoming, somewhat nosey, but with a sufficient sense of humor to laugh at almost anything. Soon enough I warmed up to their ways. That summer, and the next one, I spent hot days lounging in Bilha's house, both of us snacking on cookies in our underwear. Bilha and I discussed politics only obliquely, but when we did, she betrayed an obvious sense of compassion toward both Palestinians and Israeli victims of terrorist attacks. She often said things like, "What a mess we are in."

I was so flush with the excitement of my first international vacation, the culture shock, and meeting my in-laws that I couldn't even begin to question the information I absorbed from my new family. I knew about the conflict, but like many Americans, I had already been programmed to believe that Arabs tend toward terrorism. There was a conspicuous blank spot in my mind regarding what it is the Israeli military does. I had been bombarded my entire life with images of Palestinian militants, but I had never seen an Israeli soldier in action. Media had taught me that Israel was the weary victim of constant Palestinian attacks and the lack of any representation of an Israeli response indicated that Israel was constantly on the verge of being conquered. By the time I met Carmel, I was hearing whispers of Israel's security measures: a wall, for instance; an image of a tank rolling through a Palestinian village as kuffiyeh-clad Palestinians threw Molotov cocktails at it. Later I would learn that these "security measures" had killed four times as many Palestinians as terrorist attacks had killed Israelis. The statistics about children are especially disheartening. According to Israeli human rights organization B'Tselem, eight times more Palestinian children are killed as Israeli children. Carmel had made jokes about how Arabs have so many more children anyway. One such joke went, "How long does it take an Arab woman to take out the trash? Nine months." In the US, Carmel acted as a representative of his country by making racist jokes he didn't really believe. In Israel, with his family, there was no need.

They were proudly smolanim, lefty, but no Israeli escapes what one of my Israeli friends call "the Zionist propaganda." They lamented the tough treatment of the Palestinians but believed it was all for the purpose of defense. They freely condemned settlers and right-wingers, who believe all of historic Palestine should be under Israeli control, but fiercely defended their country's actions against outsider criticisms. Visitors to Israel, recent immigrants, and natives are all subject to the same narrow "Israel experience." Birthright tours emphasize Jewish history and Israel's many achievements while ignoring the price Palestinians have paid.

Attendees of Zionist high schools in Israel (which most public schools are) are not taught about the Nakbah, or catastrophe, that accompanied the creation of the Jewish state. Their history books jump from the Holocaust to the birth of Israel, leaving out the expulsion of hundreds of thousands of Palestinians and the massacres of whole villages in 1948. Israeli culture overall (as well as its mass media) minimizes Palestinian suffering while overemphasizing Palestinian violence toward Israelis—then minimizing Israeli violence toward Palestinians.

I knew that a piece of the puzzle was missing. As a critical thinker, I could not believe that the Palestinians would continually subject *themselves* to a cycle of violence that ripped families apart and deprived them of their homes and livelihoods. Would any of us give up our lives, our own children's lives, if we had any alternative?

I had been trying to find the missing piece of the puzzle, and I had learned what questions to ask. I was also learning Hebrew. Half my friends were Israeli. I was accepted as one of them, even as a celebrated member. Bilha was so proud of me, she would broadcast my every accomplishment to all her friends. My crowning achievement was being on the front page of *Ha'aretz* newspaper, the biggest left-leaning paper in Israel. I was photographed watching the flames caused by a Gazan missile. The newspaper photograph became a symbol of my level of understanding of their situation. There was proof that I had seen with my own eyes how they suffer. I had been initiated. Henceforth, I received less criticism for my association with Palestinians.

I decided that I needed to visit some actual Palestinians, ones who were *currently* living in the West Bank. I would have to see for myself. I wanted to see what Palestinian culture was like, apart from the conflict.

I had talked to Palestinian friends in the US They helped me arrange a visit to the West Bank. I spoke to a friend of a friend on the phone and organized my bus rides so I could meet him in Ramallah. This man had asked that I call him Mr. T, because his first name starts with T and he wished to remain anonymous. When I laughed about the name, his lack of familiarity with this American TV character just reinforced the difference between Western and Palestinian culture.

My in-laws were afraid for me. They insisted I call them at least twice a day. Carmel told me stories about Israelis who had ventured into the territories and been murdered. His stories had only the weight of anecdote—the way a shark attack is a gruesome idea, but most people don't consider it a pressing concern. It felt even as distant as a folktale or a mother's dispensing of conventional wisdom. Take your medicine. I wondered if Israeli soldiers were given this medicine before an operation in the West Bank or Gaza. I stuck with my plan, against their advice.

Mr. T met me at the bus stop, and I only knew him because he was waving at me. Before I arrived, I had asked him on the phone, "but how will you find me?" He only laughed. Now I knew: I was certainly the only American tourist there. Mr. T approached and took my hand. My first impression was that he resembled my high-school civics teacher.

Mr. T has a background in international law (which he says has no practical application in the Occupied Territories) and works for two non-profits in Ramallah, both of which are concerned with Palestinian culture and refugees. He took me to the Jalazun refugee camp, just North of Ramallah, which is home to some 12,000 people, mostly from cities in the interior of Israel, such as Ramla and Lod. During and after the 1948 war, they were expelled from their villages and moved into refugee camps elsewhere in Israel, Gaza, the West Bank, and surrounding Arab countries. As we walked through the narrow streets, he explained that Israel has legal control over the camp, under the Oslo Accords, but that all services (sanitation, health, education) are provided by UNRWA (United Nations Reliefs and Works Agency). However, Mr. T says these services have been declining since the establishment of the Palestinian Authority (PA). Since UNRWA was established to care for Palestinian refugees, the Oslo Accords were seen as The Beginning of the End to the refugee problem. If the Palestinians had their own government, they could provide their own services. But the PA has had its hands tied since its inception and has not been able to mature enough as a governing body to be able to provide those much-needed services.

The streets of Jalazun show myriad signs of poverty: graffiti, garbage, crumbling walls, poorly-paved, narrow roads, and empty lots filled with trash. There is no grass anywhere, except where it grows from amidst the rubble. Mr. T points these lots out here and there and says these homes were demolished by the IDF. When I ask why, he gives me an answer I will hear many, many times during this visit: "For security." He says it with a sad sort of chuckle and when the look on my face prompts him for a more complete answer, he adds, "That's what they say. That's what they always say."

The school for boys sits at the edge of the camp, behind which one can see the characteristic red-tiled roofs of an Israeli settlement. Mr. T tells me that the water supply to the camp is sometimes withheld, for three days per week during the summer, and that Israel does not permit either the Palestinian Authority or UNRWA to dig wells below a certain depth. I have asked several people why this is, and naturally, I get different answers from Israelis and Palestinians. My husband explained that if dug improperly or too deeply, a well can pierce an underground aquifer and taint other wells with salinated water. Mr. T said he had not heard that but instead was told that Palestinian wells could not be dug deeper than Israeli wells in the same area. In any case, Israel has control of the area's water resources and Israeli settlements nearby enjoy swimming pools while their Palestinian neighbors sometimes cannot even take baths.

Mr. T welcomed me into his home and provided everything I needed—food, shelter, company—for the three days and two nights I stayed there. I was unsure about host/guest protocol at first, so when he ordered and paid for my carrot juice at a juice bar, I asked him how much it was as I pulled out my wallet. He gave me The Look. I had become very familiar with The Look during my time in Israel. It is one of the many cultural aspects Israelis and Palestinians have in common. It says, "What, you're trying to *pay*? Oh, do put that away, it's a pathetic attempt."

Hosting, in Palestine, seems to be even more of a high honor than it is in Israel, which is something I never thought possible, since Israelis had been the most welcoming and thoughtful people I had yet encountered. Although, when I really examine my life experience, I should have realized that it is not those who have most who are the most generous. Just after high school, I used to babysit at hotels for tourists. Almost invariably, the guests at the most expensive hotels, with the largest rooms, tipped the worst. Guests at the Best Western tipped better than guests at the Ritz.

And so it was that a man who lives with his parents and eight siblings in a refugee camp purchased everything I needed during my visit.

I quickly found that Palestinian culture could not be separated from the conflict. The Palestinian people feel its effects every day. It governs everything they do, every decision they make. How many young people have decided not to go to college because the nearest university is on the other side of a checkpoint? How many mothers have decided to let their children go hungry for a night rather than go out to buy food during a curfew? How many doctors have had to decide which patient needs medicine more badly when there is not enough for both?

Unlike the plain exteriors of the houses in Jalazun, the insides had been thoughtfully decorated. Mr. T's contained matched furniture and drapes, and sets of knick-knacks proudly stood guard in each corner. The home included a large family room, a sitting room, a kitchen, bathroom, and several bedrooms. I asked Mr. T why there was such a big difference between the outsides and the insides of Jalazun homes. I had wondered if the residents of the camp did not own their houses. Maybe the IDF did not allow them or UNRWA to make improvements to the infrastructure of the camp. But Mr. T's answer was much simpler. He quoted Palestinian poet Mahmoud Darwish: "We enjoy life whenever we can."

After this, we walked to the camp's gathering place and smoked a hookah and talked about many things. I asked him another question, one I had asked many people during my stay in Israel. What is the difference between a terrorist organization and a political party?

Mr. T thought quietly, then said, "My own view is that terrorism does not have a definition so far. Under any circumstances, conflicting parties do not have to target a civilian population. But at the same time, if an occupying power oppresses an occupied people all the time and does not leave them any other option, then their action would be violent. I'm not trying to justify suicide bombings. But at the same time I can tell you that I understand them. Because if you hit me, if you continue hitting me, you have to expect my reaction. You are telling me, 'Come and hit me back.'"

He thought a moment more and then added, "One night about two years ago, there was a knock at the door. It was two a.m. Some soldiers came into the house and made me stand there, and took a picture of me. There was no reason for this. I believe this is terror."

An Arabic radio broadcast came on, discussing the prisoner swap between Israel and Hezbollah. Israel received the bodies of two soldiers abducted two years ago in exchange for five of Hezbollah's soldiers, who had been held in Israeli prisons for many years. I asked Mr. T if he thought it was fair to exchange five live prisoners for two dead bodies. He said, flatly, "yes."

I pressed him, "Do you know what crimes the prisoners were held for?"

"No, I do not."

"So how do you know it's fair?"

"If this is the only way Israel will release them, what difference does it make?"

This led to a discussion of Israeli prisons. I asked him if he was ever in an Israeli jail and he said that he was once, for two weeks. When I asked him what the charge was, he said that he was not charged at all.

A Palestinian home reduced to rubble by the IDF

Since the beginning of the Second Intifada, 40,000 Palestinians have been arrested, according to the Palestinian Central Bureau of Statistics. Prisoners can be held on "administrative detention" for years without being charged, and then released inexplicably. Other methods of punishment are house demolition, crop burning, and deportation. All these actions can take place without charges being brought. According to the organization If Americans Knew, of the 9,000 Palestinian prisoners held by Israel in December of 2004, 4,000 had not had a trial.

Palestinian children over age 12 are considered adults in the military courts in which they are tried for crimes like stone throwing. This law is different than the Israeli civilian justice system, in which Jewish youth are considered adults at age 18. One former child prisoner I interviewed said the typical stretch for a 14-year-old stone thrower is six months. Statistics released by The Palestine Center indicate that the years between 2000 and 2006 saw the arrest of 4,000 Palestinian children. At the time their brief was released in April of 2006, 330 children were in custody, which constitutes 3.5% of political prisoners held by Israel. 70 of those children were found to be ill "due to the lack of basic medical attention."

* * *

The next day, Mr. T brought me to Jericho. We saw Hisham's Palace, the archaeological remains of a winter palace from the Umayyad Caliphate. As we sat quietly in the shade of a public park trying to cope with the heat of the day, Mr. T said, "You know, things in the Arab world are changing. It will not benefit Israel to continue acting this way. Before two years ago, before the Second Lebanon War, the world believed Israel was a superpower that could not be defeated. That is changing."

The next morning, I began the five-hour journey back to Tel Aviv. My mother-in-law, who had been strongly opposed to my trip, was waiting for me, and I sat wearily on her plush sofa, enjoying the cool, air-conditioned house. She said the phone had been ringing off the hook with inquiries about my trip to the other side. Despite her interest and rapid-fire questions, I quickly found that any statement I made was met with defensiveness. Bombed out civilian homes? *The United States bombed civilian areas in Yugoslavia in 1999, why doesn't the world cry about this?* Palestinian prisoners tortured in Israeli jails? *No, our prisons are like Club Med for those terrorists, they get an education and... well, your country has used torture, why point the finger at us? What was the point of going there, of placing yourself in danger?*

What I thought, but did not say, was that the point was simply to know the truth. The truth is where it all begins. But the truth is a cold rock in the belly that most Israelis cannot digest.

Good Germans

By Emma Rosenthal

I. Year: 1969

"*Good Germans,*" my father muttered as we walked from door to door petition in hand, collecting signatures, working for an end to the war in Vietnam. Some yelled at us to "go back to Russia!" Others politely said they didn't want to make waves, cause a problem.

"What do you mean Daddy, how do you know they are German?" I asked, only ten years old, not yet having learned the nuance of ethnicity (these matters must be taught).

"They aren't German, Em."

"Why did you say they were *Good Germans?*"

"They," my father explained, "are like the Germans who weren't Nazis. They did not profit from slave labor, did not serve in the army, were just silent. *Good Germans* did not attract the attention of the authorities, pretended not to know, did not worry about the smoke, the stench. Saw Jewish girls, outside the camp, singing on their way to the factory.

"See, they are happy," they whispered.

Years later, claiming: "We had no idea."

"*Good Germans;*" Jew to Jew, this is not a compliment.

II. Year: 1977

I sit in a hotel lobby in Berlin waiting for my sister to come down from the room. A day of walking, shopping, museums, the insipid kindness of strangers giving me directions.

Peaceful, calm. Bach, not Wagner playing over the lobby hush, a place for guests, tourists, businessmen. Niceties like a tourniquet around my neck. Every man in the lobby, my father's age and German.

And I am surrounded.

Some hid Jews, falsified documents, killed one so hundreds could go free; unlikely, but perhaps one of these men was righteous.

In 1977 safety, I am caught in the possibility that perhaps, suddenly, I might find myself in 1942, surrounded. My Polish skin not sufficiently hiding my history. My foreign features betraying my identity, ancestry, difference.

The quiet peace of the hotel lobby covers the bones upon which we walk: The lives evaporated, bodies cooked to dust, skin stretched into lampshades, hair woven into rugs, ashes into the soap the *Good Germans* bathed in to wash away the stench, the soot that coated their nostrils, their skin, their cities, as they breathed in the dead cells of Jews they didn't know. The Jewish girls, dancing between the camps and the factory just relieved to be outside for the day.

"See, they are happy."

III. Year 2000

Intifada! Uprising!

Intifada! Uprising!

Who are the *Good Germans* now?

Israeli generals admit to studying Nazi strategy against the Warsaw Ghetto Uprising, the tactics to bring down the ghetto of Jewish insurrectionists fighting to the death; the suicide missions of desperation by those who had nothing left to lose, holding back the Nazis longer than all of Poland.

I hear of Israeli soldiers marking numbers on the arms of Palestinian prisoners

rounding up all the men
torture
targeting children
house arrest
refugee camps
checkpoints
collective punishment
house demolitions
ex-judicial executions
high officials calling the people "vermin"
"a cancer
not enough chemotherapy"
"transfer"
(the final solution).
And the silence, the complicity.

I have met these people, all of them; the *Good Germans* and the generals, the soldiers who just want to get through the tour alive so they can get a job when they get out. The Palestinian families who want to send the children off to school, pick the olives, turn the key in the door to the house that no longer stands in the village that no longer exists beyond the rubble covered in the pine trees planted by collections taken in Diaspora synagogues: the forestation of the desert. The hope of Europe's refugees: the invisible destruction of a homeland.

This strange apartheid: the mythical connection to a land but not the people.

The imposition of dominion behind the veil of blood and myth.

Oppressed turned oppressor, consciousness obscured by this twist of history, this betrayal of memory, this strange apartheid, fought on the backs of children and the bellies of women. An intricate labyrinth of false distinctions, of exclusive roads, checkpoints and confiscations.

Hidden by tanks, barricades, checkpoints and armor, we think we are different.

Guns poised, sights set on the image,

We look in the mirror: the distorted likeness.

Or are we the image shooting the reflection?

This is no ancient mythic battle.

There are no city walls,

No Midianite virgins

No skin of wine nor loaf of bread.

Just perhaps the two sons, Isaac and Ishmael sacrificed by the father, reunited upon his death

And the women, Sarah and Hagar, pitched in voiceless struggle, breast against breast

For land, bread, water and wombs.

Parched throats seek a hidden well. Tired hands plow a field from bitter dirt. Oranges and olives provide a defiant harvest.

And I know this is not my home

and

it is not my war

and

if it were my war

I could not fight!

The land is not for sale or plunder. Nothing can be gained from hegemony. In this betrayal of our history, killing them is killing me.

We have broken the mirror of our own souls and we have broken it upon their backs.

The Monsters are Taking Over

By Alice Rothchild

At the end of October 2007, I am one of a group of delegates from a US health and human rights project touring East Jerusalem with Angela Godfrey-Goldstein. Angela, the Action Advocacy Officer of the Israel Committee Against House Demolitions (ICAHD), speaks as the van winds its way around the ancient city. First, she gives us some background about herself and her involvement in anti-occupation political activism. Angela was born in England, lived in colonial Africa as a child, and was educated at an English boarding school. She lived in South Africa for five years, working in Soweto in the anti-apartheid struggle, and then moved to Israel.

As she explains the rapidly progressing project to transform Jerusalem from a shared, open city to a predominantly Jewish one, I take out my tape recorder hoping to capture her stream of comments. Angela's on-the-ground narration is punctuated by an urgent sense of outrage and supported by elaborate maps and a flood of convoluted details. She wants us to understand Jewish settlement expansion in East Jerusalem and the three main settlement blocs, Gush Etzion to the south, Ariel to the north, and Ma'ale Adumim to the east, and the impact of these growing Jewish population centers on Palestinians. She outlines on the map where old and new Jewish settlements are growing, steadily creeping into Palestinian areas and notes that the open spaces contain former Palestinian villages such as Deir Yassin and Lifta that were destroyed in 1948. Angela reports that open green spaces are sometimes re-zoned and then become land for settler development with "only 12 percent of annexed East Jerusalem zoned for Palestinian residential purposes." Because much of that land is already built upon, Palestinians in East Jerusalem are facing a huge shortfall in housing and a dramatic rise in land and housing prices. As if this all weren't enough, Angela tells us that it has always been virtually impossible for a Palestinian to obtain a building permit.

Additionally, there are serious inequities in the system. The 240,000 Palestinians in East Jerusalem represent approximately one-third of the entire Jerusalem population; one-third are Israeli West Jerusalemites and the other third are Jewish settlers in East Jerusalem. However, Palestinians receive less than 10 percent on average of the Jerusalem municipal budget. The implications are enormous: two percent of the municipal budget is allotted to Palestinian cultural affairs, 15 percent for education, there is usually little to no garbage collection in East Jerusalem, no postal delivery, and poorly maintained sewage, water, and electrical systems. Half the homes in Palestinian East Jerusalem have no running water but depend on pirated supplies coming across the roofs from neighbors who must be paid expensively. Palestinians must hook up phone lines individually without the supportive infrastructure that caters to the needs of Jewish residents. There are thirty-six municipal swimming pools in West Jerusalem and zero in East Jerusalem.

Angela says: "People say for their municipal taxes all they get are bulldozers." At the same time, with the restrictions created by the eight-meter-high concrete separation wall snaking through neighborhoods, many returning East Jerusalemites are not only renting expensive apartments but also paying off vacated properties they built in nearby neighborhoods that are now on the wrong side of the wall.

While I had understood that in the Occupied Territories more and more Jewish settlements are being built in order to merge into larger blocs, isolating and crippling Palestinian neighborhoods, I was unaware of the intricacies and magnitude of the project. Later, I found a 2005 article by Jon Elmer of *The New Standard* that quotes a *Christian Science Monitor* article from 2003. After a 25 year history of Israeli settlement building and an expanding Greater Jerusalem, Uri Bank of the right-wing Moledet Party laid out his strategy for Jerusalem just as Angela had described:

> "'We break up Arab continuity and their claim to East Jerusalem by putting in isolated islands of Jewish presence in areas of Arab population... Then we definitely try to put these together to form our own continuity. It is like Legos: you put the pieces out there and connect the dots. That is Zionism. That is the way the State of Israel was built. Our eventual goal is Jewish continuity in all of Jerusalem... Everything that goes on in East Jerusalem is a microcosm of what goes on in Judea [and] Samaria,' referring to the West Bank with the term preferred by Israelis who consider the territory to be part of Greater Israel."

We tumble out of the van onto a bustling, sandy street with the Golden Dome and ancient walls of the Old City as the backdrop, and a cascade of Palestinian homes in the East Jerusalem neighborhood of Silwan. We are greeted by honking traffic, crowds of women in head scarves, scruffy laborers, bearded men wearing yarmulkes and *tzitziot*, and bright-eyed Israeli recruits. I notice the site of an archaeological dig, Israeli flags draped over scattered homes on the hill, and a tourist garden claiming this fragment of the Holy City as the ancient City of David. At each Jewish site we see fortifications, security fences, armed guards, and often the blue and white Israeli flag, which feels like a symbol of aggression, of deliberate provocation. Angela explains that now extremist Jewish settlers claim this area as Jewish land.

With my tape recorder in hand, I listen to Angela explain a bit of convoluted recent history. A court decision ordered the Jewish settlers to leave. They didn't, and in fact, the settlers received a retroactive building permit, "and that's why you see these new flags on it celebrating their presence." There are currently 50 settlement compounds "and a taxi driver recently told me many more Palestinians have quietly sold and left." At the same time, at the bottom of the valley, 88 Palestinian homes are under demolition orders which cannot be appealed in court because of Regulation 201, which allows Israel to control areas of national importance. This regulation has apparently been resurrected for this purpose, having last been used when Israel demolished all the houses in the Mughrabi Quarter of the Old City in 1967 to make the Wailing Wall plaza. Meanwhile, I learn from the ICAHD there are more than 45 Jewish buildings and institutions in the Muslim and Christian quarters in the Old City, (the most famous being the home of Ariel Sharon), as well as a plan to build 33 more Jewish residential units in the Muslim Quarter.

I am beginning to share Angela's sense of outrage as I collect the details of this unfolding tragedy. I learn that the "Judaization" of East Jerusalem is made possible through the active collusion of right-wing Jewish settlers and the Israeli government with the support of academics and foreign entrepreneurs sharing a messianic as well as nationalistic vision. For example, Elad, an extremist Israeli settler organization, was hired as a subcontractor in 1998 by the Israel Nature and National Parks Protection Authority and the Jerusalem Municipality to run The City of David national park and archaeological excavations. Significant financial backing comes from Christian Zionists as well as wealthy Jews. A particularly egregious player is Irving Moskowitz, a US physician, bingo and gambling magnate, whom right-wing settlers refer to as "the savior of Jerusalem." He funds the City of David national park, the Beit Orot settlement on the Mount of Olives, and developed the Ma'ale Zeitim settlement at Ras al-Amud in East Jerusalem. He also plans to build the Kidmat Zion settlement at Abu Dis, inside East Jerusalem. Elad secretly purchases Palestinian homes in and around East Jerusalem using front organizations that appear to be Arab, and then rapidly flips the property to its ideological Jewish settlers, often arranging new construction and infusions of militant settlers at particularly sensitive political moments. His foundation is also an avid supporter of American Friends of Ateret Cohanim, a group of militant Jews who believe that Jews should be in sole control of the Old City and should rebuild the Old Temple on the site of the Dome of the Rock and the Al-Aqsa Mosque.

Moskowitz additionally earmarks millions of dollars for militant settler religious schools most analogous to the extremist madrassas and recruitment centers in the Islamic world. These messianic, ideologically-driven young Jewish students, like their counterparts in Hebron and other Jewish settlements driven by religious entitlement, are often violent and determined to create a large Jewish presence in Palestinian areas.

As the tour continues, we pass the gardens of Gethsemane, the Church of All Nations, Church of Mary Magdalene, and "Dominus Flevit, which means 'Jesus wept,' because that's where he was in Gethsemane the night before he was taken away." At the top of a hill, across the street from the City of David park and visitors' center, Angela points out a dusty archaeological excavation site marked by an Israeli flag. A number of archeologists and societies have been highly critical of this excavation effort, which not only threatens more Palestinian home demolitions and results in intimidation and questionable land practices, but also focuses on proving a Jewish claim to this area to the exclusion of thousands of years of subsequent history, according to a 2008 article in *The Chronicle of Higher Education* by Yigal Bronner and Neve Gordon. This highly sensitive project is in search of evidence of the Old Testament's King David and the Judean Kingdom, while ignoring artifacts from other cultures and violating the ethical foundations of archaeological research.

"In terms of archaeology," Angela explains with a sense of outrage and irony, "they're doing exactly the opposite [of an ethical investigation]: they're smashing through all of the years until they get to where they want to be, not interested in what happened before or after... The business of trying to get all the Palestinians out of the Silwan area, that's so political because it goes beyond just the archeology, it's also about isolating the Old City and preventing even East Jerusalemites from getting to places like the Al-Aqsa Mosque."

I ask, "Why is there so little effort to stop these projects, which seem unethical and politically explosive?" According to Angela, there is a lack of awareness among Israelis as well as a fear of ideological settler violence if confronted with an opposing viewpoint.

"There's an Israeli way of keeping your head down and just getting on with life. 'What do I care? I can't solve it. It's too big,' and we get used to things, we normalize them, so we stop seeing how abnormal it all is." I ask her what led to her own political transformation. She explains that she shifted from environmental activism to human rights after working with Bedouins in an agricultural cooperative and handicrafts outlet for women.

"And that's really what changed me as your average Israeli, because first of all I learnt Arabic, I learnt to be comfortable in Arab culture, and started to see things from outside, as opposed to inside Israel... That sort of made me more the type of person who looks around and says, 'Somebody's got to do this stuff,' because I saw that nobody else would or could. And increasingly there comes the point of responsibility where, if you are reasonably strong and reasonably disciplined, you understand."

As I look at the men with automatic rifles, both military and private security forces, either casually walking among the crowds or positioned combat-style at an entryway, I try to imagine what it would be like to be a Palestinian family living under these conditions and what happens when a family cannot tolerate this any further. Angela offers her thoughts:

"A hundred Palestinians are squatting in a building next to the American Colony Hotel, because they refuse to be forced out of the city. But you see you have here Al-Aqsa Mosque increasingly being isolated." Besides restricting and controlling Palestinians, "it's all very illegal and very shady and I think it is creating a huge rift in Israel because there is huge corruption, there is massive immorality... How do you explain away the Palestinians living on that land? These so-called religious people don't intend to share; they certainly don't recognize the sacred in all of life. The leadership of these particular settlers is religious, these tend to be religious Zionists: many of the Orthodox, they want Jerusalem as the Holy of Holies, whereas the religious Zionists want Greater Israel. On the other hand, some of them are militants who are working to get Jerusalem, the Temple Mount, the Second Temple, all of that. I don't deny their connection with the land. I don't deny the right of Israel to exist and the need for Israel. But I do deny the tactics of creating terror, the tactics that are not prepared to share, or do not see the sacred in all life and the need for peace and to open the heart. A journalist said to me the other day, he was talking to one of the top Israelis... he said to him, 'Have you ever considered a policy of generosity?' He didn't know what to say. Of course they never do.

"So they're not prepared to acknowledge the others' traditions, rights, and existence. They want it to be exclusive. I think that is also very danger-ous because if you don't have borders to your behavior or your country, and everything is allowed and you just want to keep pushing and pushing, you become somebody who is a pusher. You become a monster. And that I think is where we've gone since the assassination in 1995 of Yitzhak Rabin. The monsters are taking over."

We are back in the van, traveling through a maze of superhighways and tunnel systems, heading towards Ma'ale Adumim, a community of 35,000 stretching eastward from Jerusalem like a bubble toward Jericho, surrounded by the growing separation wall. Ma'ale Adumim is affordable, clean, quiet, well-kept and ten minutes from Jerusalem via a tunnel under Mount Scopus. According to a recent Peace Now report, 86 percent of the settlement is built on privately-owned Palestinian land, much of it captured during the 1967 Six Day War and seized for "security." The settle-ment established in 1975 also resulted in the expulsion of the Bedouin Jahalin tribe and, according to Angela as well as the Israeli journalist, Gideon Levy, the majority of the Jahalin have since been forced to live in the area of the Abu Dis garbage dump or eke out a miserable existence in the area of the Judean Desert around Ma'ale Adumim. Furthering this indignity, 3,000 Bedouins have now been given military eviction orders because they live inside the route of the Wall that will soon completely surround Ma'ale Adumim. This mounting injustice has been well docu-mented by ICAHD as well as a U.K.-based group of professionals called Architects and Planners for Justice in Palestine.

As we enter the community, I am immediately struck by an ancient, gnarled olive tree gracing a traffic roundabout. Where did it come from? "Recently replanted here and you'll see others as we go in, absolutely stolen, no doubt about it," Angela tells me. "Israel is even exporting Palestinian olive trees, or selling them in North Tel Aviv to yuppies for

$8,000." Settlers use five to six times as much water as Palestinians in this area and twice as much as Israelis within the '67 borders, so extensive irrigation has turned the greenery lush and extravagant. Angela further clarifies that Palestinians do not have water sold to them by Israel at agricultural rates, so they actually pay three times the amount as their Jewish neighbors. She adds, though it is becoming quite obvious, "the water is being used for political purposes."

The message to the Jewish inhabitants here is clearly that this is a comfortable and permanent garden suburb just like any other Israeli community. We pass a modern-looking school, a community hall, a museum and one of the four municipal swimming pools surrounded by rows of palm trees, exuberant green grass, and another ancient olive tree in a traffic circle. We gaze at a gushing, waterfall fountain graced by huge abstract white concrete doves near the local library, "The Library of Peace." This time, Angela is silent; the irony hangs as thick as the hot Jerusalem air.

As the tour continues, and we drive by miles of apartments, city buildings, and shopping centers, Angela tells us that over the next few years, the population is expected to double and that housing to accommodate 70,000 people has already been built. She says people talk of having one million Jews living in this area, and an airport has also been planned.

"They have been building in the last five years, during the years of the Road Map Israel signed," she says. She is referring to the US-backed Road Map in which Israel agreed to "freeze all settlement building including natural expansion." She adds that Ma'ale Adumim is only building on 10 percent of its land, so there is 90 percent to consider for future development. "Then [someone like] Tony Blair says we have to get back to the Road Map... As if we were ever in it."

I am astonished at how extensive and substantial Ma'ale Adumim appears, neighborhood after neighborhood wrapping over multiple hilltops, huge industrial parks, even a technical college for pilots and astronauts. People are attracted here by tax breaks, subsidies, incentives, "and people are coming here from Jerusalem because it is quiet and clean, and near to work—and no pesky Arabs around. It's a nice place to live. In fact, the last American ambassador's brother lives here."

As we leave, we look across the un-irrigated, brown Judean landscape towards the vast industrial area. Beyond the municipal boundary, we spot the caravans and trailers creeping along hilltops, joining Ma'ale Adumim to create a massive wedge from Jerusalem to Jericho, bisecting the West Bank, north from south, East Jerusalem from Ramallah and Bethlehem. Because Jerusalem represents 40 percent of the Palestinian economy, taking and developing the land east of the Holy City—and further isolating Jerusalem from the West Bank—politically and economically destroys the future of Palestine. Raffi Berg, of *BBC News*, calls Ma'ale Adumim "Israel's 'linchpin' settlement."

Angela notes that most people in Ma'ale Adumim move here for economic reasons, and "they don't see themselves as a problem for peace. They don't see the strategic political geography of where they are. They just think they are near Jerusalem, it's no big problem. They're peaceful people. They wouldn't understand that this is really the nail in the coffin of the two-state solution and the most dangerous settlement as to Palestinian viability."

Angela grabs a map and points to an irregular tract of land northeast of Jerusalem. As we look, she plunges into a description about a thorny controversy called E1. "And now as we go back in I'm going to point out to you, I can see it behind there. As we go into Jerusalem you'll see it better, the police station that is just now being finished on E1. It's over there at 10 o'clock in the middle of that hill. Can you see below the Mount Scopus tower? As we go up there you will see that huge building, three rectangles."

There is a tendency for my brain to glaze over when faced with complicated maps of this area with their crazy quilt of boundaries and walls, villages and settlements, bypass roads, seam zones, red dashed lines projecting future construction. Angela insists this detail is important to understand: E1 or Area East 1 Plan was initially proposed to establish a massive 12 square kilometer development between Jerusalem and Ma'ale Adumim. This development would further isolate East Jerusalem and effectively destroy the possibility of a contiguous Palestinian state with East Jerusalem as the capital. It would consolidate an ever-expanding

Israeli border and create a larger buffer zone. With further research, I find that in 1994, the Israeli government confiscated this hilly area from Palestinian villages with no compensation to the inhabitants and with the intention of building 3,500 more settlement homes for approximately 25,000 new residents This plan was opposed not only by Israeli peace groups such as ICAHD and Ir Amim, City of Nations, but also by the US government. Ir Amim, represented by Danny Seidman, took the case to the Israeli Supreme Court.

"The answer of the state and the settlers together has been to build two humongous police stations on E1," Angela says, "which they say is for security, and get away with it that way, with a six-lane highway and so forth. The earlier police station is in full use. The second one is not yet inaugurated, but it's less than one month away from being finished. I was on its roof only a few days ago. The road hasn't yet been finished and it's costing taxpayers $13 million. The police station itself is being built with settler money. Ten million dollars funded by the settlers, because the settlers are thereby buying a police station elsewhere, next to the Moskowitz settlement in Ras al-Amud. They're saying, 'OK, we want this police station, and in exchange we will build another one for the State, on E1.' So now there are two enormous police stations on E1, and that undermines the Palestinians' ability to develop there themselves."

Angela reveals that once the police have moved into the police stations in E1, the settlers will move into the vacated police station on the Mount of Olives, so they will control access in the direction of the Old City.

Earlier in the day, on our winding drive down the Old Jericho Road, we'd seen the current police station, a sleepy building with three or four officers milling about, and many parked cars. It's the central headquarters for Judea and Samaria police, and the riot police have a small office there.

Angela now explains: "The building they have built instead of it is just phenomenal, it's bigger than the national headquarters of the police... They're planning for militarism. They're planning for taking control and certainly planning to get away with it, and they've already done it, so there's not much the Palestinians can do. And as far as showing the intentions of the State of Israel, you can see there's no recognition of the possibility that all this infrastructure will ever have to be dismantled. On the contrary, like the wall, it's all so vast and expensive that it's almost bound to be permanent."

As we approach the monstrous police station on the hill, we see Bedouins that have been forced to move due to the construction. Angela emphasizes that these Bedouins are farming at a deficit, giving animals dry feed because they have lost their grazing area and do not want to change their traditional lifestyle. Of course, she adds sadly, "They do not enjoy living in shacks and would prefer to be living in a house with electricity and water." These people are originally refugees forced out of the Negev in the 1940s and 1950s and given West Bank ID cards.

"Sometimes they were forced at gunpoint, forced to sign that they left of their own accord. And the guy that was in charge of the military intelligence and later Military Governor of the West Bank after 1967, when he then 'transferred' more than 100,000 Palestinians by bus out to Jordan, was Chaim Herzog who went on to be UN ambassador for Israel and then became President of the State."

With the Israeli intention to ultimately develop E1 and the inclusion of all this territory within a large loop on the Israeli side of the separation wall, travel for Palestinians has also become increasingly challenging. Angela says the army recently proposed a road for Palestinians, called "the life line," which will go in a wide eastward loop around Ma'ale Adumim, turning a 20 minute drive into an hour long trek. Increasingly, with the growing settlements, bypass roads, and multiple checkpoints, it is very difficult for Palestinians to travel.

"It therefore takes twice as much time, three times as much fuel, very bad, winding mountain roads. It prevents the East Jerusalemites from getting out to Jericho or Jordan or the Hajj in Saudi Arabia. It also prevents people from being able to get into Jerusalem, because now you have the wall and checkpoints and an Israeli commercial road system and all of those settlements in East Jerusalem."

She notes that even George Bush said, "Islands won't work. They need territorial contiguity." The answer has been a maze of tunnels and overpasses. "'They will have transport contiguity.' That's what Sharon said."

I thought we had long since left Ma'ale Adumim and was surprised when Angela stops and points: "That's the other police station over there. You'll see it in a minute. It's huge and it's all on E1, and by the way, we're still in Ma'ale Adumim. If you look up the road ahead, you'll see a little sign by the side of the road saying 'Welcome to Jerusalem,' so now we are leaving Ma'ale Adumim."

I thought I understood the realities on the ground, but it seems there is no end to the depth of my astonishment and sense of despair. I have often been told that Israelis need this extensive system of control over Palestinians because of the horrendous risk of suicide bombings; this is all about security. Inherent in this statement is the implicit assumption that Israelis seek peace but Palestinians are violent and unreasonable by nature. Angela is quick to remind us that, actually, the suicide bombings started in response to the massacre at the Ibrahimi Mosque (the Cave of the Patriarchs), in Hebron, when Baruch Goldstein killed 29 Palestinians praying during Ramadan. She notes that because Rabin was afraid of revenge attacks, he placed a total curfew on Palestinians, and ultimately Palestinians were forced out of their marketplace in the Old City into an area called H1.

"So the Palestinians paid the price for that attack and Rabin funked it when he could have got all of those 400 settlers out of the Old City of Hebron," she says. "He was scared of a civil war." She told me she believes that the threat of civil war was again not substantiated during the Gaza withdrawal, thus for her "the ultra-right, it's full of sound and fury, but actually, they are not really the major problem. I think more the problem is the nature of middle consensus."

In other words, she believes most Israelis feel that each side has to compromise, but there is little attention to the actual details of the arrangement. She warns, "If the Palestinians do not have a viable state, they cannot be at peace with us, and I think then we will go into an official state of apartheid." She quickly adds that she is not against a two-state solution:

"I would love to have a viable Palestine. Voila! You know, I'm praying for miracles. But it's not any longer doable because of the facts on the ground, because the political will is absent, because no money is being talked about in large enough sums to move those settlers out. We are talking about a one-state solution, presumably, or other solutions, whatever anybody wants to get creative about. But I think the people who are going for a two-state solution are people who are going for a non-viable Palestine that will inevitably turn into one state." As someone who has lived in Israel for 27 years, she says she understands the emotional "red lines."

Destroyed Palestinian home next to new Jewish construction.

"People tell me that if you bring the refugees back into Israel you will be telling Israelis basically, that they will have to go back to Poland and the pogroms. That's how they translate it." She keeps telling her friends that they need to know the other side, to learn Arabic, to not only meet people on a social basis, but to struggle and work together. She speaks carefully into my microphone.

"It has to be really strengthening the moderates or the people who want peace, and understanding the thinking of the more extreme. Because frankly, I don't believe that Hamas is such a big problem. Most of them are intelligent people who have been left with few options. Sometimes you come across someone working with Hamas, and they look you very long and hard in the eye, and it's more or less saying, 'What else do you expect us to do, just collapse and accept whatever you say? We have to try to get some future here.' Having lived in Egypt, I also understand very clearly that the Arab world does not want to be westernized. They do not want to just give up on their culture and their ways and traditions. It's something that they have to deal with.

"And we have to demilitarize in order to stabilize the whole region; Israelis really don't get the fact that as a nuclear power, we're a cause of stress on the whole region. And while people may get short-term advantages from using armed struggle or military violence, ultimately it has far too high a price-tag; it really ends up being self-destructive. But we've never given peace a chance. Never treated the Palestinians as equals with historic rights, never defined what real security implies. Or normalcy."

We are heading back down Jericho Road, one of the main highways linking Jerusalem to the West Bank as well as the main road to Jordan, Saudi Arabia, and in the old days, Iraq and Kuwait. Suddenly, we turn a corner and are faced with a massive 24-foot concrete wall, a loop of the separation wall that winds its way through the neighborhoods of East Jerusalem. The barrier completely obstructs this once significant roadway, destroying what was a thriving commercial neighborhood.

We park at a gas station and Hassan, a warm, weary smile emerging from the creased lines of his face, comes out of his shop to greet us. We learn that because of this location, he used to have an excellent business, next to the most popular gas station in Palestine, but now his thriving business has died.

Hassan explains, "I don't go outside Jerusalem because I can't take my wife or my children. [Occasionally] maybe to Ramallah or Jericho, some place where they can play without paying any money." He comments that he has to pay the city 8,500 shekels, more than $2,000 a year, but he has almost no income. "I want to pay [less tax] but they said, 'No.'" He looks up at an imaginary adversary and declares, "You destroy my life, you destroy my fields, my dream, I don't know."

Angela points to an area up a hill where a settlement is planned, "and it means that very soon they're going to have a lot of settlers going past here so you don't know what is in the future." Hassan responds that he has visited America, likes America, but he is worried about survival. He notes ironically that there are organizations to "go help the fish in the sea, but the Palestinians are killed here, they are destroyed here, and nobody helps them. It's a shame for all the world. I am sorry."

We wander through his tiny, dusty corner store, buying water and sesame bars, and learn that the wall started in 2002 as smaller square blocks which were replaced gradually in 2004 with the massive concrete slabs. More recently, a wire fence was added on the top to stop young people from climbing over. Hassan mentions that he met Angela when she was one of the first people to write graffiti on the wall.

I say, "Yes, I remember a well-known photo of a large spray-painted scrawl, 'Welcome to Ghetto Abu Dis.'" It turns out that was Angela's work.

"I was writing this graffiti here, 'Welcome to Ghetto Abu Dis,' and there was a border policeman on the roof here and some more over there and I had just done some other graffiti on the other side and come around. I saw them there so I knew I had to go very fast, so I just wrote very fast. They kept telling me to stop and I went faster and then they came and took the can out of my hands. So instead of 'Abu Dis' it said 'Abu D,' and then later, on another occasion, I filled in the 'Dis.' They took me away for questioning. They said they might judge me with incitement, that's with a prison sentence."

She says she wasn't scared, but she wanted to be very clear that the route of the wall was unfair; it was placing people in closed off ghettos, separating Palestinians from their families, their hospitals, and ultimately increasing the risk of terror attacks. She describes taking a group of 175 Palestinian children who were too young to need permits, getting permission for the teachers from "a really nice border police officer," and loading up five buses for a field trip. These children had never seen the sights of Jerusalem, had never seen the flower beds beautifying Ma'ale Adumim. They were thrilled by the lions, giraffes, and elephants in the zoo and years later still recount this magical trip. "They were out of prison for a day. When we came back, all the people watching us come, these five coaches full of children, and they were like, 'How did you do it? How did you get out of prison?'"

We depart the store and head back to the patio restaurant of the Jerusalem Hotel, where we'd first met. The hotel is a former Arab mansion built of cream-colored, thick blocks of stone with graceful arches and a lush traditional ambience, 100 meters from the Damascus Gate. Before we disperse, Angela says she has one last quote for us. Apparently, when Angela Merkel, the German Chancellor, came to Israel, "she wrote in the guest book of *Yad Vashem*, [the Holocaust museum]: 'Maturity comes from acknowledging responsibility for the past.'

"OK, that, coming from a German, in Yad Vashem, is a powerful statement," Angela says. " But ... is she trying to tell us something? Maybe she was. I hope she was."

Loved
is a Person

By Osie Gabriel Adelfang

My family left Israel for the US in 1974, when I was eight. Every summer until I was grown, I went to visit and stayed with my maternal aunt's family. Her children—my cousins—and I were very close, although their family was devoutly Orthodox while mine was as secular as you can get. Each summer, I hung out with my close-in-age girl cousins, leaving my liberal B'nai B'rith youth group in Rochester, New York, for the religious, gender-segregated B'nai Akiva summer scout activities in Jerusalem.

I must have been 14 the summer the girls refused to join me at the "mixed" pool so as not to expose their bodies to men. Which is why I was at the Jerusalem Hilton Hotel pool with my 10-year-old boy cousin, Haim. As we dressed to leave the pool, I was still blown away that the little kid I'd never much noticed had gone along with my "let's sneak in without paying" scheme as though he did that kind of thing all the time. I grabbed my skirt off the back of the deck chair and pulled it on over my swimsuit. Haim put on shorts and a t-shirt, using his left hand to do the work that his right, injured at birth because of a doctor's error, could not do. I noticed, but did not comment on, the fact that he did not replace the yarmulke he had taken off to swim.

I had a startling thought, which I remember as clearly today as if I were still sitting on that plastic pool chair on that hot, dusty Jerusalem afternoon. The thought was: "He's going to be my favorite, forever. And he's going to be a rebel—and no way religious." Haim now thinks this is a funny story, because he remembers the pool but does not remember the yarmulke part, which ended badly when his ultra-religious-private-school teacher happened to board the bus and saw his bare head sitting next to an immodestly dressed teenage girl (me). He reached that strong left hand into his shorts pocket fast as lightning and threw the yarmulke on, quickly fastening its attached bobby pin. He did not, himself, know he was going to end up living a secular life, or rebel in a truly meaningful way, until many years later.

Although our time at the pool marked the beginning of our friendship, I had, of course, known him his whole life. I saw him all those summers: the sweet toddler with long, golden-curls (which were cut off, in the Orthodox tradition, when he was three); the annoying little brother pestering us older girls. But I have another, earlier memory of Haim, too. It is, perhaps, my own first memory.

I was four, dressed in my favorite green dress and red patent-leather party shoes. Standing in the courtyard of an old Jerusalem building, my girl cousins and I watched the action inside. The party, we knew, was a celebration of Haim's birth, and the festivities were well underway. We had a large family, and he was the first male grandchild, the prodigal son. Music played, and men in black coats danced around the room. Someone called us in, and the dancers began to throw candy high in the air. My cousins and I ran through the room, collecting candy in the fronts of our dresses. At some point, the children were sent outside again. I sat on a low stone wall in the courtyard and closed my eyes, savoring the sticky, sweet-and-sour combination in my mouth. My ears were filled with the din of adult voices raised in celebration. But suddenly, an unexpected noise jolted me: the sound of a baby crying. Not seeing my cousins, I followed the sound to the silky white bassinet set in the corner of the room. It must have been as tall as I, because I had to reach up on my tiptoes to see in. And the sight shocked me. There in the white bed was my tiny new cousin, wailing at the top of his lungs. At his midsection, a white cloth diaper was soaked in a widening circle of blood. I turned to get help, but no one paid any attention. It came to me with a start that it wasn't that they hadn't heard, it was that they knew and didn't care. In my child's mind, I realized that in some major way, the sweetness of the candy, the music, the dancing, and the grownups' joy was not in spite of, but because of, the bleeding infant in the bassinet.

Years after the swimming pool incident, when Haim gave up the yarmulke for good, he was serving as a tank commander in the IDF. Because of the bad right arm, the military did not want to put him into combat when he was drafted. But Haim, a proud Israeli boy raised on the tradition of independence and self-defense, wanted to serve where it counted. He wanted to protect his country. He fought the bureaucracy—and hard—for his right to do so. He finally won. I was vaguely aware of his life, but at that time I was busy living a hellacious first marriage and sometimes following the Grateful Dead. Israel and my cousins were far away.

Haim served during the First Intifada, and by the next time we met, in 1995, he was not a boy at all but a 26-year-old man, and I was a jaded but much happier divorced woman. Over drinks, cigarettes, and calamari—in a Jerusalem bar! On Shabbat! How times change!—he told me about his service and about the Intifada. Yitzhak Rabin had just been assassinated by a young Orthodox man opposed to the peace process, and the country was reeling, grief mixed with continued hope for the process. My body warmed by glasses of red wine, I felt my heart fill with pride and love for Haim as he talked about the growing peace movement. He was so passionate and optimistic. He told me the Intifada was like Israel's Viet Nam, that it had taught the country that occupation would not work. He had already refused to serve his twice-yearly reserve duty in the Occupied Territories, unwilling to "shoot rubber bullets at children," as he put it. At that time, his refusal was by personal request. He asked his commanders, and they assigned him elsewhere. I remember that Jerusalem night clearly, too, his steady arm around me as we walked home through ancient streets, and I remember thinking: "I was right about him all those years ago!"

And then I went back to my life and he to his. Jewish-American friends were shocked at my story. How could an Israeli refuse to serve his country? Israel was "ours," the Palestinians (and the Arab nations that supported them) were the enemy, trying to wipe us out as the Nazis almost had. These friends were hesitant about the peace process underway at the time and continued to support Israel unilaterally with their voices and their money, answering my questions by reminding me once and again that supporting Israel is "what Jewish people do."

The Oslo accords happened, and peace did not come. I saw my cousin Haim twice in the interim. He came all the way to Alabama for my second wedding, and then he let my new husband and me stay at his place on our Israeli honeymoon in late 1998.

A few months later, I was pregnant with my first child. We chose not to find out the gender, to be surprised. Reading through my pregnancy and childbirth books, I reached the part about newborn circumcision, and something didn't seem right. I didn't connect my discomfort with my cousin at the time, though I still held the memory of that long-ago party. But I began to research the practice of circumcision, and the more I read, the more I questioned.

I knew that circumcision had been part of Judaism since its beginnings, since Abraham circumcised his son in exchange for God's promise. But now I read that even in those times, only a small piece of the foreskin was removed, far different from today's practice. It turns out that through the ages, the ritual has not always been practiced by Jews (even Moses, who brought us the Ten Commandments, did not circumcise his son, I was surprised to learn). And I now knew that contrary to popular belief, a boy must not be circumcised to be Jewish. According to Jewish law, he must simply be born of a Jewish mother.

Also contrary to common wisdom, circumcision is not a routine, safe and relatively painless procedure. The foreskin is not merely an "extra" piece of skin; it serves to protect the glans from abrasion and keeps it in its natural state: a sensitive mucus membrane, not the dry, thick one it becomes on a circumcised penis.

In the Jewish tradition of *Brit Milah*, the *Mohel* first inserts a probe around the glans, to separate the foreskin from it. He then pulls the foreskin through a clamp, squeezing and cutting it off (alternately, the procedure can be completed with a knife and no clamp, allowing for no protection for the glans and for the religiously required bleeding). I realized, as I read, that this was what had happened to my wailing cousin that day we celebrated his birth.

Circumcision, whether performed in a hospital or by a *Mohel*, can cause myriad complications, including infection, hemorrhage, surgical injury, or even death. With all these facts—even the American Pediatric Association's official policy does not advocate routine infant circumcision—how could it be that secular Jews, those of us who don't keep kosher, don't pray Jewish prayers, don't attend synagogue or keep the Sabbath, how could it be that this is the one practice we all still adhere to? With so many laws of Biblical times long since discarded (animal sacrifices, stoning, polygamy) why did we keep this one thing? Something we do to our helpless sons, without their permission, without much forethought at all, because that is "what Jewish people do?"

My husband and I decided against circumcision if our child was to be a boy. Our daughter was born January 9, 2000. We named her Anna—for Anna Gabriel, my great-grandmother who died in the Holocaust.

While Anna was enjoying the first year of life in the peaceful suburbs of America, the Second Intifada began in Israel/Palestine. Haim and I kept in touch sporadically. He called me long-distance several times during my complicated second pregnancy; he called again to comfort me when my daughter, Erika, was born and died on May 6, 2001. And then, almost a year later, he called once more. This time, he needed a favor.

The situation in the territories had deteriorated further, enough that a group of 50 IDF reservists and combat soldiers had written "The Combatants' Letter." The letter states, in part, that they would henceforth "not continue to fight this War of the Settlements... not continue to fight beyond the 1967 borders in order to dominate, expel, starve and humiliate an entire people."

Haim had signed the letter and became active in the group, Courage to Refuse. He told me that out of respect for his commanding officer and his men, he had written his own letter to explain his actions. He needed my help in translating the letter into English so he could submit it to the UK's *Guardian of London* newspaper.

I quickly learned that speaking two languages does not make you a translator. Getting the words right, along with the tone and intent, took almost a week, as well as help from my father and extensive use of the Hebrew-English dictionary. I was humbled to help him, he had put his livelihood and his freedom on the line to do what was right, all I had to give was a few words. I hope I did justice to the passion of his Hebrew letter when I wrote:

"...By including the concept of "a clearly illegal command" in the code of military law, [Israel] has obliged its soldiers to refuse to carry out orders that are immoral or opposed to the values on which a democracy is based... The most critical question that arises is "what exactly is an illegal command?"...An order to fire on a child standing before a roadblock is clearly illegal. But if the order is to shoot above his head to chase him from the roadblock, does the emotional damage the shooting causes the child make the order illegal? Is it illegal to continually enter Palestinian citizens' homes in the middle of the night? Is it illegal to prevent the free movement of Palestinian citizens? Aren't the searches, the humiliation, our many mistakes, an indication that our treatment of the Palestinian population under our rule is clearly illegal?

"Military law does not define what a clearly illegal order is, but leaves it to the soldier. My interpretation of the law... includes any command that, when obeyed, leads to humiliating human beings, robbing them of self-respect, and depriving them of the basic human rights protected under the UN declaration of human rights, a document signed by Israel...

"Prohibiting Palestinians from traveling along roads without providing alternative routes, the never-ending delays at roadblocks, the many hours required to travel short distances, the humiliation, the destruction of homes, the incessant searches, the need to aim weapons at innocent women and children—all these actions turn the IDF into an immoral occupying force, and in these I refuse to participate...

"In addition to the great harm we are causing daily to Palestinians, we damage ourselves as a society. Our society is based on moral precepts in Judaism, which states that "loved is a person created in God's image." Instead, we are raising a generation of violent young people immune to pain and human suffering, a generation who don't see in the Palestinian a human being, only part of a mass to be avoided and feared."

The translated letter was published in the *Guardian of London* May 6, 2002, which would have been my daughter Erika's first birthday.

I had another, healthy, baby girl, Ellie, in 2003. We were once again spared the pressure, the unsolicited comments, and the derision that would have come had we had to explain our anti-circumcision stance.

Then, in 2007, we adopted a boy, Sasha, who came to us from Russia intact, just as God had created him. I have learned in the adoption community that, most often, American parents (Jewish or not) decide to circumcise their internationally adopted child. When Sasha first came to us, he was two. In the first year or so after he arrived, when I dressed him at the pool or changed his diaper in a public restroom, I often saw shock, even revulsion, in people's faces as a response to my beautiful boy's body. Their eyes (and sometimes mouths) told me this wasn't what they expected or approved of. My son is two years older now, and my rebellion of refusing to cut him is no longer seen or commented on by others (although his mother continues to speak out, with her words most often falling on deaf ears).

In the meantime, the fight continues for the soldiers in Israel who refuse. Six hundred eighty-eight have signed the original Courage to Refuse petition. Many others have less publicly refused. The support petition has almost 15,000 signatures to date. More than 280 members of Courage to Refuse have been court-martialed and jailed for their refusal, although the Israeli government can only make examples of a few, lest it be known that thousands of its own citizens are imprisoned in protest against its policies. That truth might be a little too much for even the most loyal Jewish Americans to hear.

It makes me sad for myself and for all of us when Jewish Americans do not stand against inflicting pain in the name of Judaism. Too many of us, even progressives who question so much, turn a blind eye when it comes to the accepted Jewish-American worldview, as if any questioning, any disloyalty, would just provide an opening for a past, present, or future enemy. For me, my Jewish identity can't exist apart from my belief that

God made our sons' bodies perfect the day they are born. And my love for the beautiful land where I was born (my family, the warm desert breeze, the rows of eucalyptus trees, the noise, the candor, the people who look like me) cannot exist apart from facing these truths about atrocities being committed in the name of "my" homeland.

This is a story, partly, of helplessness: as a child I could not lessen my cousin's pain. As an adult, I could do no more than give him some English words. And I feel helpless to stop the Israeli occupation or the practice of routine infant circumcision. But for me, this story is also a lesson in courage and hope, a lesson my cousin continues to teach me. If Judaism is based on the moral precept that "loved is a person created in God's image," then it is our duty to speak up, to refuse to inflict pain on the innocent, because we are all created in God's image.

In response to his protest, the IDF simply stopped calling Haim for reserve duty. My cousin is now a professor, husband, and father of three girls. He says he's glad he was able to avoid having to make the circumcision decision himself. He surprised me by saying he thinks it is because of the brutality, not despite it, that fathers continue to subject their sons to this rite of passage into Jewish manhood. I imagine that having seen men inflict violence on the helpless much more often and up close than I have, he may unfortunately be right in this regard. Haim is still active in the peace movement, and is a member of the joint Israeli/Palestinian group Combatants for Peace. He and his Palestinian "enemies" have put down their weapons to talk, get to know each other as human beings, and promote peace. Many years after he accompanied me to the Hilton Hotel pool, he has truly become not just my favorite, but my hero.

January 2008: The Tightening Noose
Gaza under Hamas, Gaza under Siege

By Jen Marlowe

Previously published online at tomsdispatch.com

Images from Rafah flicker on my computer screen. Gazans are blowing up chunks of the wall that stood between them and Egypt, punching holes in the largest open-air prison in the world, and streaming across the border in an incredible refusal to submit.

I learn via email that my friend Khaled Nasrallah rented a truck in order to drive food and medicine from Egypt into the Gaza Strip. He was acting for no humanitarian organization. He's just a resident of Rafah, a Palestinian town which borders Egypt, with a deep need to help and an opportunity to seize.

Rarely do our media offer images so laden with the palpable despair that has become daily life in the Gaza Strip. The situation has bordered on desperate since the outbreak of the Second Intifada in October 2000, when Gazans could no longer work inside Israel and the attacks and incursions of Israel's military, the IDF, became a regular occurrence. Closures on the Strip progressively intensified.

On January 25, 2006, Hamas, an acronym for "The Islamic Resistance Movement," won the Palestinian Authority parliamentary elections, defeating the reigning secular, nationalist Fatah Party. Israel, the United States, and the European Union all refused to recognize the new Hamas government and many elements within Fatah also went to great lengths to ensure it failed.

Tension and violence mounted between the Palestinian factions, culminating June 2007 in Hamas' takeover of the Gaza Strip. Israel responded by sealing the Strip. On September 19, following the repeated firing of crude Qassam rockets from the Beit Hanoun neighborhood in the northern Gaza Strip into the Israeli town of Sderot, the Israeli government unanimously labeled all of Gaza a "hostile entity." Since then, restrictions by the IDF on whom and what is permitted to enter Gaza have grown harsher still. There are not many witnesses to testify to the plight of Gazans these days. I was lucky: In early January, in order to visit the participants of a peace-building program I once worked for, I got in.

It was a brief visit, so I didn't stroll down largely empty supermarket aisles or visit hospitals to check on which supplies were unavailable. Instead, I used the time to talk to Gazans involved in responding to the international siege and the internal crisis that had led to it.

There were even rare moments when the dual crises faded into the background, such as the afternoon when I drank coffee in Rafah with Khaled Nasrallah, his brother Dr. Samir Nasrallah, and their wives and children. Rachel Corrie, a 23 year-old peace-and-justice activist from Olympia, Washington, had been killed on March 16, 2003, while standing in front of their home trying to prevent its demolition by an Israeli military bulldozer. Between October 2000 and October 2004, the IDF destroyed 2,500 homes in the Gaza Strip. Nearly two-thirds of them, like the Nasrallahs', had been the homes of refugees in Rafah.

Now double refugees, like so many residents of Rafah, they ushered me into the living room of the apartment they have occupied since their home was destroyed in 2004. It was sparsely furnished, but the family's spirit more than compensated. When, for instance, thin, quiet Dr. Samir saw an opportunity to make his young daughters or nieces smile, his own face lit up. He clowned around as pictures were taken, encouraging the girls to find ever sillier poses.

Only as I was leaving did the siege make its presence felt. I pulled a few chocolate bars and a carton of Lucky Strikes from my backpack, saying, "I understand these are hard to find these days."

Dr. Samir accepted the gifts with an odd solemnity. He then unwrapped a single bar of chocolate, carefully broke it into small pieces and distributed a section to each of the little girls. With an equal sense of gravity, they sat on the thin, foam mats that lined the room, slowly biting off tiny pieces, letting the chocolate melt in their mouths. They were still sucking on the final bits as I said goodbye.

* * *

When I first learned I had permission to enter Gaza, I wondered what I should bring with me. How much could I carry? What did a people under siege need most? I imagined filling my backpack with bags of rice, coffee, sugar, beans—until I called my friend Ra'ed in Beit Hanoun.

"Hey, Ra'ed. I'm coming to Gaza on Wednesday. What can I bring you?"

There was a short pause. "Can you bring cigarettes? Lucky Strikes?"

Requests from other friends started coming in. Could I bring a carton of Marlboros? Viceroy Lights? Rania requested chocolate. Ahmad asked for shampoo.

There was something tragic and yet comic in these requests. Were they a sign that the situation wasn't as desperate as I feared? Or maybe, given the sustained stress Gazans have been enduring, the need for psychological relief took priority even over the staples of survival.

Ra'ed called back with an additional request. "Can you bring one of those rechargeable fluorescent lights? The power's being cut off now for eight hours at a time and my kids have exams. They can't study without light."

Erez border is the only crossing point for internationals entering the Gaza Strip. The border between Rafah and Egypt had been sealed since the Hamas takeover. I arrived at Erez, struggling with my three brimming bags and two rechargeable lights. The terminal had been completely rebuilt since my last visit a year ago. The modest building housing a few soldiers and computers was gone; in its place was a slick, spotlessly clean, all-glass complex. It felt as though I were entering the headquarters atrium of a multi-million-dollar corporation.

My passport stamped, I continued along a maze of one-way revolving gates. Crossing through the final gate, I found myself in Gaza, the sleek glass building and its sanitized version of the Israeli occupation suddenly no more than a surreal memory. I was on a cracked cement pathway, covered by dilapidated plastic roofing, in the middle of an abandoned field of stones and rubble. Realities, even small ones, change so quickly, so grimly, here.

*   *   *

Soon, I was in Ra'ed's car heading south to Rafah with Rania Kharma, a coordinator for the Palestinian-International Campaign to End the Siege on Gaza. I handed her the chocolate bars she had requested. "Thanks, *habibti* [my dear]" she said. "You know how important chocolate can be for a woman." Normally remarkably passionate, Rania now spoke and moved with the air of someone smothered by wet blankets.

We passed carts piled with bananas and oranges. "So there's fruit here. What exactly is getting in?" I asked.

Before the siege, she explained, 9,000 different items were allowed into Gaza. Now, the Israelis had reduced what could enter the Strip to 20 items or, in some cases, types of items. Twenty items to meet the needs of nearly 1.5 million people. It felt like some kind of TV fantasy exercise in survival: *You're going to a deserted island and you can only bring 20 things with you. What would you bring?*

Medicine was on the list, Rania told me, but only pre-approved drugs registered with the Israeli Ministry of Health. Frozen meat was permitted, but fresh meat wasn't (and there was a shortage of livestock in Gaza). Fruits and vegetables were allowed in, but—Ra'ed quickly inserted—less than what the population needed and of an inferior quality. It was, he felt, as if Israel were dumping produce not fit for its citizens or for international export into Gaza.

Diapers and toilet paper were allowed entry, as were sugar, salt, flour, milk, and eggs. Soap yes, but laundry detergent, shampoo, or other cleaning products weren't.

"I'm not sure about baby formula," Rania said. "Sometimes you can find it, sometimes you can't."

Tunnels under the Egyptian border, once used mainly to smuggle weapons into the Strip, were now responsible for a brisk black market trade. Hamas, which controlled the tunnels, reportedly earns a hefty profit from the $10 it now costs Gazans to buy a single pack of cigarettes. Chocolate couldn't be found, not even on the black market. A bag of cement that once cost about $10 reached $75, and, by the time of my visit, couldn't be found at all. All construction and most repair jobs had ground to a halt.

The Ramadan fast is traditionally broken with a dried date. A special request for dates was made to the Israelis and granted—but only as a substitute for salt. To get their Ramadan dates, Gazans had to sacrifice something else.

"Israel says they're not going to starve us," Rania remarked with a wry grin as we neared Rafah. "They're just putting us on a really tight diet."

I was traveling to Rafah in order to purchase handmade embroidery from the Women's Union Association, a women's fair-trade collective. I planned to bring the embroidery back to the US for the Olympia-Rafah Sister City Project, initiated after the death of Rachel Corrie and working to realize her vision of connecting the two communities.

Rafah's economy was once based on agriculture and on the resale of goods from Egypt, according to Samira, the energetic program director of the association. Over the past seven years, however, most of the orchards and greenhouses in the town had been uprooted by Israeli military bulldozers. Then, once the siege began for real, Rafah's merchants could no longer obtain goods from Egypt. By the time I arrived, only about 15 percent of the population was working, most employed in government ministries.

Samira brought out a large plastic bag brimming with embroidered work. I fingered beautiful shawls and wall hangings as she eagerly described an exhibition of the women's hand embroidery held in Cairo last May. Every piece had sold. The women had then stitched new pillowcases, bags, and vests at a frenetic pace for an exhibition in Vienna scheduled for September 2007. The Gaza Strip, however, was sealed in June. Neither the women, nor their embroidery, could leave. That plastic bag contained what should have gone to Vienna. The project had already come to a standstill as the necessary raw materials, chiefly colored thread, were now unavailable. Once these pieces were sold, nothing would be left.

Samira encouraged Rania to try on a stunning, exquisitely stitched jacket, its joyous blaze of color strangely out of place in that bare office. It had taken a year to complete, she said proudly. I hesitated to buy it. It felt wrong, somehow, to remove that splash of color from decimated Rafah. But who else would be arriving in Rafah soon to buy from the collective? I asked Samira to prioritize which items she wanted me to purchase. She packed up the jacket and as many other pieces as I could afford in that same plastic bag, and handed them to me.

While Ra'ed and Rania argued energetically in Arabic on the drive back to Gaza City, I stared out the window, noting the green Hamas flags and banners that decorated nearly every street corner and intersection. As we neared our destination, I asked Rania if she wanted to join me that evening.

"I'd love to, *habibti*, but I have to get back to my apartment before 6:30. The electricity will be cut after that and then—no elevator. I live on the ninth floor and, since my knee injury a few years ago, it's really painful to walk up all those stairs."

* * *

My next stop was the Al Mezan Center for Human Rights. Mahmoud Abo Rahma, a young man with intense green eyes, spent much of our time together discussing Gaza's acute electricity crisis. Israel's fuel restrictions were his primary concern. It wasn't just transportation that suffered when fuel was sanctioned, he explained. Without fuel for Gaza's sole power plant, the ensuing electricity shortage constrains health and education services, leading to an acute humanitarian crisis.

Mahmoud broke the situation down, jotting figures and connective arrows on a small sticky pad. Gaza needs 237 megawatts of electricity a day, 120 megawatts of which are supplied directly by Israel. The Gaza power plant used to supply 90 megawatts, which meant the Strip remained 27 megawatts a day short, even in what passed for "good times." Then, in June 2006 after the kidnapping of Israeli soldier Gilad Shalit, the Israelis bombed the power plant, truncating its capacity. With the siege and its acute fuel shortage, the plant could generate even less. Mahmoud feared that it might have to stop operating altogether. On top of this, he added, Israel was threatening to curtail the electricity it provides.

Sixty-eight people, he said, had already died as a result of the sanctions. Others had certainly suffered siege-related deaths in which multiple factors were involved. For those 68, however, a clear red line could be drawn directly to the siege—to disruptions in critical services or to the simple fact that someone couldn't reach Israel or Egypt for needed medical care unavailable in Gaza.

As I left his office for my next appointment, my mind wandered from the 68 extreme cases to the thousands of day-to-day small sufferings that have become part of the fabric of life for Gazans. I imagined the Nasrallah family huddled under blankets trying to keep warm without a functioning electric heater, or Ra'ed's children studying for exams by candle or flashlight, or Rania climbing those nine flights of stairs on an injured knee.

* * *

Suhail is the director of the Rachel Corrie Cultural Center for Children and Youth in Rafah and its sister center in Jabalya Refugee Camp. Both centers are under the umbrella of the Union of Health Workers. "We are sometimes asked," Suhail told me, "how a children's center fits under the umbrella of a health organization, but the connection is very clear. According to the World Health Organization, health is not measured only by lack of illness. A healthy child is also healthy socially, emotionally, and mentally—and this is the role we play."

He talked about the many obstacles the centers face. "Our activities are designed to help support children mentally, emotionally, but they don't want to leave the house. The kids are depressed. Everyone is depressed."

In 2005, the teens who made up the center's *dabke* troupe—*dabke* is a traditional Palestinian folk-dance—traveled to Britain, touring and performing in 15 cities. Now, they can't leave the Gaza Strip. "We want Al Jazeera to broadcast them performing in a local celebration," Suhail said. "The youth[s] are also making their own movies, showing their daily realities."

His parting words echoed in my mind: "There are different ways to break a siege."

*   *   *

At the pristine offices of the Gaza Community Mental Health Program (GCMHP), Husam al Nounou and Dr. Ahmad Abu Tawahina brought into focus the degree to which the Hamas takeover had affected life in Gaza. Husam, the program's director of public relations, was soft-spoken and Dr. Abu Tawahina, its director general, was animated; both men radiated self-assurance and dignity.

By then, the large-scale, bloody political violence between Hamas and Fatah militants had ended. There were no longer shoot-outs on street corners. Military actions against Fatah-connected individuals were ongoing, however. Dr. Abu Tawahina described cases of people leaving their houses only to find the body of a relative dumped on the street, or frantic Gazans calling police stations after a family member "disappeared," only to be told that there was "no information."

The margins of free speech, never wide in Gaza, had decreased significantly, Husam told me. Direct or indirect messages of fear and intimidation are now regularly passed on to journalists and human-rights workers. Fatah affiliates are beaten up, detained, their cars burned; Fatah-related organizations have been totally destroyed. I was reminded of Mahmoud's reply when I asked him if Al Mezan's ability to work, exposing human rights abuses to the people of Gaza, has been affected since the takeover.

"We are not changing our work at all," he said, choosing his words slowly. "We are not allowing ourselves to be intimidated."

Ideological and political differences between the movements have certainly played a major role in the internal fighting, Dr. Abu Tawahina carefully explained, as has the regional factor: Washington supports Fatah, while Hamas is backed by Syria and Iran. But, as Husam pointed out, other factors should not be ignored. "There is no tradition of democracy or transfer of power in Palestinian society," he said. "Fatah was not prepared to lose the January 2006 elections or give authority over to Hamas." The situation is exacerbated by the adamant refusal of both the US and Israeli governments to recognize the democratically elected Hamas government, as well as their support for Fatah's attempts to sabotage it.

Dr. Abu Tawahina explained his understanding of what has transpired: Many Fatah officials had spent years in Israeli prisons, he commented, enduring torture at the hands of Israeli interrogators and soldiers. After signing the Oslo peace agreements in 1993, members of the Palestine Liberation Organization (in which Fatah is the most powerful faction) were permitted to establish a self-governing apparatus called the Palestinian Authority (PA). Israel put pressure on the PA to arrest those who opposed the Oslo process, particularly when opposition groups carried out attacks in Israel.

As a result, thousands of Hamas members, most of whom had not been involved in the violence, spent time in PA jails. Fatah interrogators then applied the same techniques to the prisoners in their hands as the Israelis had once used against them, even ramping the methods up a notch or two.

Now, the very people Fatah abused in prison are in charge in the Gaza Strip, and they are seeking revenge for a decade of mistreatment under Fatah. The phenomenon can be found in Gazan civil society as well. One hundred thousand Palestinian laborers used to work inside

Israel, suffering daily humiliations at the hands of Israeli soldiers at the Erez crossing. If they directed their anger and frustration at their abusers, they would lose the permits that allowed them to work inside Israel. Instead, many erupted in rage at home at their wives or children, creating new victims.

* * *

Because of an ever more traumatized population, the mental health program's services are desperately needed. The staff work feverishly, trying to develop new techniques to meet the catastrophe that is Gaza, but nothing—not telephone counseling, nor bringing in other NGOs, nor holding community meetings to give larger numbers of people coping tools—can meet the escalating needs of the community.

"Peace is crucial for mental health services," Dr. Abu Tawahina said pointedly. "Our staff feels inadequate in helping our clients. When the source of someone's mental symptoms comes from physical needs not being met, then there is very little that therapeutic techniques can do."

"The level of hate towards those behind the siege—Israelis and Americans—is increasing," Husam said. "We need to show the human face of people from the US"

His comment reminded me that Samira and Suhail had also spoken about their desire to launch an Internet program between young people in Rafah and teenagers in Olympia, Washington, Rachel Corrie's hometown. In itself, there was nothing shocking about the fact that anger towards Americans, whose government strongly supported the siege and had also backed Fatah in the internecine struggle in Gaza, was on the rise. If anything, what was surprising, touching, and human was the urge of a few Palestinians to challenge that hatred and put a human face on Americans.

* * *

Now, back in the US, I stare at those images from just a few weeks ago of Gazans flooding into Egypt. I feel myself on some threshold between paralysis and hope—anguished by the unending desperation that led to the destruction of that wall and yet inspired by the way the Gazans briefly broke their own siege.

What we are allowing to occur in Gaza—and we are allowing, even facilitating, it—will come back to haunt us. Still, despite all the indicators of a society locked into an open-air prison giving in to violence and possibly fragmenting internally past the point of reconciliation, I hold on to a small hope. Perhaps those of us outside that prison will be affected by more than the explosive rage that inevitably comes from an effort to collectively crush 1.5 million people into submission. Perhaps we will also be affected by the Gazans who refuse to submit to their oppressors, be they from outside or within. Ultimately, I hope we'll choose to stand in solidarity with them.

Sunset Undone (ghazal)

By Kim Goldberg

January 12, 2009
    I tilt my way down melting streets, each slippery step undone
by icy wind and gutter slush. Winter's snowy heft undone.

Numb fingers grump inside wool gloves, lamenting that
abandoned mug of steamy tea—by necessity left undone.

Yet these small miseries they shame me when laid beside the truth
of blistered moonscape and blockades, a city's breath undone.

I hurry to the crossroads of colliding worlds, terminal avenue
cleaving commercial like a severed worm, soft flesh undone.

We hoist our placards high against wet gusts, chins tucked,
firm grip on simple message of life's ravelling weft undone.

I grab an "O" as we form a curbside row of alphabet-teeth, an urgen
mouth pleading "CEASEFIRE NOW," leave some shred undone.

People pass, barely glance, stretch to press the "Walk" button,
don't even know Gaza is the topic or ragged tourniquets undone.

Cars and trucks shoot by, some honk, some shout "fucking faggots!"
(Is this war's buckled root? A faulty proof of manhood best undone?)

A furtive man approaches, suggests we protest something huge
like government mind control via toaster ovens, our behest undone.

And whether it made a difference, raised awareness, sowed a seed
or two of restless thought, is anybody's educated guess undone.

All you can do is your best and then post it to Facebook. If I knew
how to drop poems not bombs on Gaza, I would know regret undone.

I will start with this poem, stuffed in some kind of bottle transformed
from its mini-mart origins and tossed toward a sunset undone.

———

* an ancient form of Arabic verse involving repetition and internal rhyme

Heresies in Pursuit of Peace

By Starhawk

April, 2002

In the ruins of Jenin, an old friend of mine is digging bodies out of the rubble where Israeli bulldozers flattened houses, burying people alive. Blackened, maggot-ridden corpses, unearthed from the rubble, are displayed to anguished relatives for identification. A teenage girl unearths an infant's arm and wonders what to do with it. A Palestinian father cries over the dark smears of flesh that once were his two little daughters. Another Jewish friend leaves an anguished message on my cell phone: "I'm in downtown Washington DC. There's a huge, pro-Israel rally going on. I don't understand it. How can Jews support this? I know you must have something inspirational to say. Send me what you write."

She doesn't know that for weeks I've been trying unsuccessfully to write something about the situation. I'm overwhelmed with accounts of the atrocities. Yet I am also haunted by images of bodies shattered at a Seder meal, at a café, a Passover drenched in a new plague of blood. I'm frightened and saddened by the real resurgence of anti-Semitism, by swastikas carried in peace marches, synagogues attacked.

A third friend, a deeply spiritual woman and longtime eco-feminist ally, sends me a copy of a letter she wrote to the President, titled, "Standing Firmly with Israel."

In no way can I stand with her. And yet I cannot simply stand against her, either.

I cannot stand with an Israel that tortures prisoners, an Israel that has mounted a restrictive and dehumanizing occupation, that has cut down ancient olive groves to destroy the livelihood of the Palestinians. This Israel is daily committing war crimes: refusing medical care to the wounded, firing on journalists and peace demonstrators, bombing civilians, destroying homes. Nor can I stand in the bloody remains of the Seder meal, among the corpses in the café, the restaurant. Yet to say, "Both sides are wrong, both sides should give up violence" is too simple. Placing the blame evenly ignores the reality that one side, the Israeli side, is the fourth largest military power in the world. It implies that the suicide bombs are something other than a direct response to calculated political assassinations and to a brutal occupation that has made life untenable for the Palestinians. For more than 50 years, the State of Israel has failed to guard and cherish the Palestinians' rights, aspirations, and hopes for an independence that could lead to peace and prosperity.

It is, on the one hand, incomprehensible to me that my friend could stand with such a regime. It's incomprehensible that the Jewish community as a whole, composed of people I know to be caring, compassionate and good, can stand behind the tanks, the bombs, the brutality.

On the other hand, I understand quite well the wrenching emotional journey that many Jews must make to admit the reality of what Israel is doing. For those of us who grew up saving our pennies to plant trees in the Galil, who, snowbound in blizzards, celebrated the New Year of the Trees timed to the blossoming of almonds in the Judean hills, who ended every Seder with the prayer "Next year in Jerusalem," no other issue is so painful and sad.

I am a Jew who has spent her adult life as a voice for a different religion, a blatant Pagan whose spirituality is attuned to the Goddess of regeneration, not the God of my fathers. To Orthodox Jews, I'm a heretic, which gives me a certain freedom to say what I think. I was born into, raised in and acculturated by the post-war Jewish community, but I have not been immersed in that world for many years. I speak from the margins of the Jewish community. But I am still a Jew, and the view from the edge can sometimes be clearer than that from the center.

The San Francisco Chronicle writes a front page story about a school in Gaza where little Palestinian children are taught to hate Jews. Although I have no reason to doubt the truth of this story, I question why the paper features it front and center with no counterbalancing tale of, say, the International Solidarity Movement where Palestinians and Jews together risk themselves in nonviolent interventions for peace. The hate is real, and the fear it engenders is also real. Yet the story makes me consider what I was taught when I myself was a child, during 10 years of Jewish education that included a teenaged summer spent on a kibbutz.

We never chanted, "Kill the Arabs" (although Israeli soccer fans have been known to do just that). We were never told in so many words, "Hate them." Rather, we learned a more subtle discounting, a not-seeing, as if the Palestinians were not full human beings but rather a minor obstacle to the fulfillment of a dream, something to be moved aside, something that didn't really count.

We were taught to be proud of the brave Zionist settlers and pioneers, the idealistic youths who fled the ghettoes and the pogroms of Europe to build a "new" land. And I am proud, still, of their experiments in new ways of living, their awareness of women's rights, their courage in leaving home and family to escape oppression. But I understand now that they did not come into an empty place. They did not come with the capability of truly seeing and respecting and honoring the people of the land. They came out of a Europe that had an unshakeable belief in its own cultural and racial superiority and had for centuries been appropriating the lands of darker peoples.

They came as the settlers came to the "New World" saying, "This land is ours by right, God gave it to us." The people who had lived there during those 2,000 years of exile were an impediment. And so began the long litany of justifications. First came the contention that the land didn't really belong to the Palestinians but to the Turks or the British. Then came the excuse that they weren't doing anything with it, they had not made the desert bloom nor drained the swamps. Above all, we held the trump card: that they hate us, they are raised to hate us, with a hate irrational, implacable, and unchangeable.

The word for this not-seeing of the other as an equal human being but only as an obstacle—or worse, evil—is racism. Yet to simply condemn Zionism as racism without acknowledging the context of centuries of racial hate against Jews from which it arose is to absolve those who have blood on their hands as well. Worse, it is to support the complacency of Jew haters and fascists who now emerge into the open again. Israel has indeed served the interests of the Western powers in subjugating the Arab world. But Israel also arose out of an oppressed people's dream of liberation. To discount the oppression, to deny the strength and the beauty of the dream of a homeland, is to miss the full tragedy of what is happening now. Unless we understand the dream, we cannot truly comprehend the nightmare.

I know what Israel meant during my childhood in the fifties. Israel was a promise to my family—still reeling in shock from the revelations of the gas chambers and the ovens, still searching for news of lost relatives. Israel was the restitution for all the losses of the Holocaust. It was the thing that restored some meaning and some hope into a world utterly shattered by evil. It was the proof that Jews were not just passive victims but actors on the screen of history, capable of fighting back, of taking charge of our own destiny. It was the one safe place, the refuge in a hostile world.

And for some, it was the answer to the anguished question, "How can I believe in God in a world in which such things can happen?" To acknowledge the truth of what Israel is now doing is to face a grief so deep and overwhelming that it seems to suck away all hope. To acknowledge Israel's atrocities is to gasp again in the suffocation chambers, to cover our faces with the ashes from the ovens and know that there is no redemption, no silver lining, no happy ending, no good and noble thing that emerged to give dignity to these deaths. There is only the terrible cycle of victims becoming victimizers, and the abused perpetuating abuse. It is to look down and see the whip in our own hands, the jackboots on our own feet.

"Don't make the Nazi connection," a Jewish peace group warns. "It only feeds the right wing."

And yet the Nazi connection begs to be made.

It is true that the Israelis have not built extermination camps. It is true, although not immediately relevant, that other people in the world besides Jews have done and are doing bad things. Other atrocities occur daily. But it is also true that to attempt to erase a people, to destroy their culture, livelihood, and pride, is genocide.

A wan young woman, looking depressed, wanders through the Justice for Palestine rally, carrying a sign that says: "My father survived Auschwitz. His parents didn't. Orphaned, he fled to Israel."

Part of the horror of Jenin lies in her father's new kinship to the teen-aged boy dug alive out of the rubble of his house where his parents and brothers and sisters now lie dead.

That parallel is a dark mirror that reveals how easily we become what we most despise. If we look into it open-eyed, we face truths so painful they make it hardly bearable to be human. For this is not just about Jews and Germans, Israelis and Palestinians; it's not about how any one people is prone to evil. It's about us all. The capacity for cruelty, for inflicting horrific harm, exists in us all. All we need is to feel threatened, and to let our fear define our enemy as less than fully human, and the horrors of hell are unleashed.

If we don't like the Nazi parallel, we must refuse to become Nazis. We must remember that the Nazis played on the German sense of deprivation and loss after World War One. We must admit that our own real victimization has not elevated us to some realm of purity and eternal innocence. We can grow beyond the propaganda we were taught and the myths of our childhood and the comfort of our chosen-ness, and we can see the Palestinians as the full human beings they are. We must do it even if doing so seems to require us to walk out again into the wilderness with no outstretched hand or hope of a promised land to guide us.

111

For if we admit the Palestinians' full humanity, if we admire their knowledge and appreciate their culture and cherish their children, then all the justifications of conquest fall away. No God, no superior virtue or inherent right, has granted us dominion. We have the land because we were able to take it.

And while that admission might seem to threaten Israel's very right to exist, it is not nearly as much of a threat as clinging to the justifications and rationalizations that prevent us from seeing the "other" as human.

For full human beings placed in a situation of utter despair may turn to suicide bombs and retribution. Human beings, humiliated beyond bearing, may turn to revenge. But full human beings are not mindless agents of hate. Given hope and dignity and a future to live for, human beings will tend to choose life. And full human beings can be reasoned with, bargained with, made peace with.

The wilderness, the desert, has always been the place where our people have heard the still, small voice of God.

Religion is supposed to call us away from our most brutal possibilities, to challenge us to act from compassion and love. Right now in the Middle East, religion is not doing its job.

I know well that to equate the actions of the Israeli government with Judaism is to risk feeding anti-Semitism and to erase the great spectrum of political and spiritual diversity that exists in the world Jewish community. And yet the question of Israel cannot be separated from Judaism. Our prayers for rain are timed to coincide with cloudbursts over the Sea of Galilee. We count the *omer*, the successive gathering in of the harvest from ancient fields bordering the Jordan. Fundamentalist Jews have established the contested settlements in the Occupied Territories and resist any concessions to the Palestinians. And the mainstream Jewish community stands firmly behind the Israeli government's rule of force.

The current crisis represents a great spiritual crisis within Judaism. I write as an admitted heretic. Yet it's clear to me that the Orthodoxies of all three Great Religions, along with atheists, pragmatists and secularists of many political persuasions, are embroiled in a blasphemy that far outweighs any naked dancing around a bonfire. They are united in the worship of the God of Force.

The God of Force says that force is the ultimate answer to every dilemma, the resolution of every conflict, the 'only thing they understand.' The God of Force makes His appearances in the Old and New Testament, the Koran, and other sacred and secular scriptures. The God of Force licenses his agents to kill, unleashes the holy war, the jihad, the crusade, the inquisition. The God of Force says, "Go unto the land and kill all the inhabitants thereof."

This God of Force is failing, but there are others to call upon. I am a polytheist; I recognize many Powers. In my view, many constellations of energies and forces in the universe arise from a deep interconnectedness and unity but have their own flavors, characters and names. One advantage of being a polytheist is that you can choose your gods or goddesses, acknowledging that bloodthirsty and cruel powers exist, but turning resolutely away from them. When God tells you to commit some horrific atrocity, you have somewhere to go for a second opinion. But monotheism is, of course, the heart and essence of Judaism as it is of Islam and Christianity. I submit that the God of Force is incompatible with the oneness of God. For if God is one, s/he must by definition be God of All, not of any one people exclusively. He cannot simultaneously encourage callousness and cruelty and be Christ the God of Love, Allah the Merciful, or El Maleh Rahamim, God Who is Filled with Compassion. And if he chooses a people, he does it in the same spirit in which my partner confides to each of his four daughters that she is his favorite.

The current situation is a call both to God and to us to evolve. Judaism has always had within it a tradition of wrestling with God, as Jacob did with the angel. It is a tradition of arguing with God, as Abraham did when God wanted to destroy Sodom and Gomorrah. To see God as fixed, eternally and unchangingly rigid is indeed to worship a graven image. Instead, we might see God as a dynamic process in which we are co-creators of the world we inhabit. We are actively engaged in shaping who God becomes.

We are commanded not to make images of God because our human imaginations are always limited and will reproduce our own faults and lacks and prejudices. God the General, God the Ruler, God the King, God the Distributor of Real Estate, God the Avenger, God of Holy War, God of Punishment, Retribution and Revenge, God Who Favors One People Above All Others, may in reality be that very idol, that truncated image, we are told to turn from. The worst heresy of all may be to limit our conception of the great force of compassion that underlies the world.

Judaism can march lockstep with the Israeli authorities deeper into the domain of force. Israel could conceivably exterminate the Palestinians utterly, and that is the trend of the current policies. Nothing less will crush their aspirations for independence and freedom. A Jewish community that supported that final solution would lose its soul and any claim to moral authority. An Israel that carried out the genocide would be no fit homeland for any person of conscience. The dream of Israel would become an utter and complete horror show. Finally, genocide would not bring security to Israel; it would simply inflame the hatred of the entire Arab world and jettison the rest of the world's support. One of the agonies in the current crisis is that nobody seems to have much hope or vision of how to resolve it. We can see where the road leads, but we don't know how to step off of it.

"If only the Palestinians would practice nonviolence, embrace the principles of Gandhi and King," I hear from some of my Jewish allies.

Of course, there are Palestinians, and Israelis, and many others who have stepped forward to be a nonviolent presence in refugee camps, who have accompanied ambulances and attempted to deliver medical supplies, who have written their own eyewitness accounts and spoken their truth.

But I find myself thinking "Wouldn't it be quicker if Gandhi or King reappeared among the Israeli leadership and their supporters? Are they not in an even better position to change this situation?"

August, 2009
In the seven years since I wrote the first version of this essay, I've made four trips to Palestine to work with the International Solidarity Movement, which supports nonviolent resistance to the Occupation. I've seen Palestinians, Israelis and Internationals stand together to resist the injustice of the Occupation and siege on Gaza. I've stayed in Palestinian

homes as they were searched by Israeli soldiers, supported the teams that were with Rachel Corrie (killed by an Israeli bulldozer driver as she attempted to stop a home demolition in Rafah) and Tom Hurndall (shot by an Israeli sniper). I've seen Israeli punk lesbians sit in council together with conservative Palestinian village elders, deliberating over how to stop the apartheid wall. Because of my work with the ISM, I have become, ironically, a Jew banned from Israel.

I've seen that there are no inherent barriers to communication and friendship between Palestinians and Israelis, once they define themselves as people working together for justice. It is the infrastructure of control and repression that breeds hate. Remove it, and the possibilities for peace and cooperation will flourish.

Those who love and care for Israel need to stand with her true interests now, by demanding an end to the occupation, an end to the siege of Gaza, the dismantling of the settlements, restitution and real justice. Those are the preconditions that will lead to true security and peace. They must pressure the United States government to stop covertly supporting and funding Israeli aggression.

The grip of the God of Force is strong. It is so strong that even though we can clearly see what the solution might be, we may despair at actually bringing it about. To pry that grip loose, we need to use all the tools of political activism—from writing letters and making phone calls to demonstrating, doing nonviolent civil disobedience, or even joining the peace witnesses on the front lines.

On a spiritual level, we can look into the dark mirror that reveals our own prejudices and reject them. We can believe that the force of intelligent, embodied love, as feminist theologian Carol Christ describes the Goddess, is indeed stronger than stupid, disembodied hate.

One last Pagan heresy is the belief that we can prod a sluggish God into producing a miracle or two by performing an action with conscious, focused intention.

So, as a spell for peace, make peace with someone you think you can't make peace with. Notice what resistance arises even at the thought. Reflect on how you build your case against your enemy, how you marshal your allies and ready your weapons. Note what it takes to give them up, what you must sacrifice and what you gain.

Maybe, in this process, we can all learn something. Maybe we can begin a turning, a transformation that will leave the God of Force starved of his blood sacrifices and burnt offerings, and feed gentler fruit to a kinder God. In this way, the children of Israel and Palestine can both grow up to enrich the land—not by the blood of corpses but by the songs of poets, the works of artists, the healing of doctors, the fruit of farmers, the knowledge of teachers, the wisdom of mystics. And this corner of land, battleground for so many years, might become for all people a place of refuge, vision and hope.

The Right to Exist

By Anna Baltzer

I left our International Women's Peace Service (IWPS) house in Haris village (Salfit Governorate, West Bank) in the afternoon and headed for the ancient city of Nablus, 10 miles away. Anywhere else, this trip would be quick, but not in Palestine. First, I tried Huwwara, the southern checkpoint into and out of Nablus city. The Israeli soldiers guarding the checkpoint refused to let me through. I was worried about getting into Nablus before dark, but I remembered IWPS's policy of not pleading with soldiers or asking for favors. The rationale is: We do not ask permission for something that is our right, and we do not validate the nonexistent authority of soldiers who are present to protect settlers in illegal colonies. We distinguish between the individual soldiers themselves and the institution they are serving and we recognize their humanity amidst the inhumanity of the Occupation, but we do not consent to their illegal actions and presence in the area.

I asked around for a service taxi to another checkpoint but was told it was too late. A young man with whom I had shared the taxi to Huwwara noticed I was stranded. He led me to a taxi full of other passengers who had been refused entry. We set off down the highway. Suddenly, on the side of the road next to a steep hill, the taxi came to a stop. Everyone hurried out, and I quickly realized that we were entering Nablus the long way, over the hills, to avoid checkpoints. We ran up to the summit and climbed over two roadblocks. There, we found a taxi waiting to take us to a nearby town, where we could find transport into Nablus. By the time we reached the city, it was dark. The young man who had aided me in my journey led me to a shared taxi bound for Balata Refugee Camp, where I was staying that night with the International Solidarity Movement (ISM). He would not take any money for my part of the journey. I insisted, but he just put his hand on his heart and smiled to say that I was most welcome, and then walked away.

Balata sees more violence and incursions than most other places in Palestine, which is evident as you walk through the camp. There are bullet holes in every house, school, and store. The children are tougher than those in other Palestinian communities, and their parents are more suspicious of outsiders. But the barrier is easily broken with a little Arabic and indication of solidarity. It was in Balata that I met Omar.

Omar is a gentle young man who works with ISM. A year and a half ago, Omar's cousin Mahmoud was shot three times by an Israeli army tank, which tore his body into four. Mahmoud had belonged to Al-Aqsa Martyrs' Brigades, the military wing of the Fatah party.

Omar told me that Mahmoud had once been a Palestinian police officer but found it impossible to be effective with constant Israeli military invasions undermining all efforts towards Palestinian self-rule. One day, Mahmoud confronted the raiding army with two friends. One was killed, and the other sent to prison for more than 20 years. After that, Mahmoud joined the Brigades.

When Omar's 18-year-old brother heard of his cousin's death, he was devastated. Five days later, he strapped a bomb to his chest and blew himself up in a city outside of Tel Aviv, killing an Israeli woman and her eighteen-month-old granddaughter.

International volunteers stay at Omar's house in Balata—not in support of what his brother did, but in protest of the demolition order threatening Omar's family's home in retaliation for the young man's crime. The Israeli army routinely demolishes the family homes of Palestinians involved in violence against Israel, even though the Fourth Geneva Convention explicitly prohibits collective punishment, and the Israeli army's own studies have shown that home demolitions are also overwhelmingly ineffective at preventing Palestinian violence. The anger they produce grossly outweighs any possible benefit.

Many sympathize with Israel's policies of collective punishment, citing the country's right to defend its own citizens. But Israel's punitive demolitions don't target criminals—they target everyone else. After the Oklahoma City bombing, did the FBI bulldoze Timothy McVeigh's home? Did they demolish the homes of his parents, and his siblings, and his cousins? Should they have? Would collective retaliation like this make people in the United States safer?

Photos of Mahmoud and Omar's brother hang on the wall in the front hall. Balata camp is covered in pictures of men and women who have been killed by Israeli forces, or who have killed themselves in attacks on Israel. They are revered and mourned by the community as martyrs, regardless of how they died. The majority are civilians who were killed during Israeli army invasions into the city. In mainstream Western media, we learn about all the individual Israelis killed by Palestinians but rarely see the faces and names of those killed on the other side, even though they are far more numerous.

Omar and I spent the evening playing Palestinian backgammon and talking. Omar told me he learned to play backgammon during his seven years in and out of Israeli jails. His first arrest was in 1985, when he was 13. He had been on his way to school when he was picked up by a Jeep and thrown in prison for six months. The soldier who arrested him claimed he had thrown a stone, but Omar insists he never threw stones. Never, that is, until after he spent six months in jail. When he was released from prison, his attitude had changed. If Israeli soldiers were free to imprison him without trial, he would have no qualms about throwing stones or Molotov cocktails. That was Omar's attitude until he started working with ISM.

ISM has a strict policy of nonviolence. I asked Omar what his family thought of ISM's strategies, and he said, "They support my nonviolent resistance work. Most of my friends do, too. The Israeli media says we are animals and killers, but they are killing us!"

Omar pointed to a crack in the ceiling.

"That is from an Israeli bomb that exploded the same night I stood at this window and watched my friend get shot on the street below. I wanted so desperately to go help him but I couldn't, because the army was shooting. I am powerless. I am part of ISM, but I cannot monitor checkpoints; I would have no effect. I cannot go to an organizational meeting next week, because there are three checkpoints between me and the meeting. With my last name, I will never make it. It is very frustrating, and as the Occupation policies become stricter, it will become harder to find people sympathetic to ISM's nonviolent strategies. Nonetheless, I believe there is still hope for a peaceful way. Even with one brother paralyzed from falling debris during a raid and another one with only eight fingers, after he lost two in the same raid. Even as I watch three of my cousins and my nephew spend their lives in prison.

"They took me to prison again recently. I was crossing a checkpoint near Nablus when a soldier asked me my name. I told him and immediately he asked me about Mahmoud: "Why did your cousin die?" he asked. I said, "Because you killed him!" The soldier told me I would go to jail because my family was dangerous. I said that I was different from my brother, but he said that I was Palestinian, and so I did not want peace. He called his men over to take me away.

"The police took me to a room where I was blindfolded and my hands were tied behind my back. Their men beat me on and off for many hours. I remember it was raining outside. When they had finished there was blood streaming down my face, so they took me to an army doctor. The doctor looked at me once and said 'no problem,' although I was badly hurt. I waited for them to take me somewhere where I could rest. Instead they took me to another room where they continued to beat me for another hour or so.

"When they had finished, they took me to a small, empty dark room with water on the floor. They left me there, shivering on the floor with blood all over my body. Occasionally, they would bring me food, but it was food not even fit for animals. I did not eat for three days. After five days in solitary confinement, the captain told me I would stay in jail for six months. When I asked why, he repeated the reasons of the first soldier: He said I was dangerous, and that even if my brother was dead, the "Arab wrath" would continue in me.

"The next six months were a living hell. If a soldier ever asks me if I prefer prison or death, I will not have to think twice. The bathrooms in jail were repulsive. Every day, we had half an hour for 30 people to use one toilet. We were all sick with not being able to go to the bathroom, and when we complained that it was not enough time, the guard told us, 'Don't worry, you can go tomorrow.'

"There were boys there only 14 years old. And there was an 80-year-old man who was very sick in bed, crying. I told the guard he needed a doctor or he was going to die. The guard answered: 'He is dangerous. If he dies, then the people of Israel will be safe.'

"One week before my prison time was finished, I could not sleep. I was tortured with fears that they would decide to keep me another six months, or worse, that they would deport me to Gaza so I could never see my family again. And then they told me I could go. It was a wonderful feeling of freedom, until the reality sank in that I was returning to life in another cage. I had gone from one prison to another, a bigger prison, called Balata. I am still in prison. We all are."

Omar is luckier than some. He was on Amnesty International's list of political prisoners until he was released. There are more than 9,000 Palestinian political prisoners being held in Israeli prisons today, about 10 percent of whom are in "administrative detention," which means they can be held without charge or trial—indefinitely. Approximately 40 percent of all Palestinian men in the Occupied Territories have been detained or imprisoned by Israel. Almost every day, I meet former prisoners. I recalled the day before, when a young man not much older than me had seen me looking confused (I was lost) and asked in English if he could help. I needed a phone, and he let me use his. I asked him where he had learned English and he said in prison in Israel. He had just been released the year before after nine years in prison, where he was held from age 18 to 27. The stories don't end; they multiply.

I asked Omar if his brother had warned him before he killed himself and others. Omar looked at me incredulously: "Are you kidding? Do you think I would have let him go?" His anger turned to tears. "I would have locked him in the house and brought him food and never let him out of my sight! He was my baby brother... And if I ever meet someone who knew what he was going to do and didn't tell me, I'll never forgive them."

I asked Omar if he wanted to tell me about his brother. He smiled and looked off into space.

"He's not my brother anymore. He's a part of me, inside of me." Omar patted his chest. "I still feel him here. He was great, very charismatic, always coming home with a new crazy hairstyle. He loved to dress up nice and wear fancy cologne and he couldn't wait to buy a car to drive the pretty girls around." Omar laughed for the first time that night. "He was the only person around who didn't smoke. He hated cigarettes, and when I smoked he would yell at me that it was bad for my health. He was so smart... A year before he died he'd finished high school and wanted to study in a university, but we didn't have the money. He had worked three years in a small hospital in Israel but lost his job when the Second Intifada started. After that, he was working odd jobs to save up the money for school. He wanted to be a doctor."

Omar turned to me with a big smile, "Thank you for asking." I smiled back, sadly. I didn't know what to say. There were no words to comfort. How could I tell him he was not alone when so much of the world has turned their backs on people with stories just like his? He kept apologizing for making me sad, which broke my heart.

I told Omar I wanted to tell him something. He listened. "I'm Jewish," I began. He looked surprised, but kept listening. "My family also has a devastating history. My grandparents were refugees from the Nazi Holocaust and most of their parents, sisters, and brothers were killed by the Nazis."

Omar shook his head slowly and spoke: "I see Sharon as a second Hitler. I hate what Sharon and the Israeli government do, but I do not hate Jews, and I do not hate you. God loves everyone: Muslims, Jews,

Wall mural depicting the systematic abuse of Palestinian prisoners in Israeli jails. (April 2007, Al Far'a Refugee Camp)

Christians, everyone. If you do good, then you go to Heaven. God doesn't distinguish and neither do I."

Omar may not distinguish, but Israeli official policy does. Balata Refugee Camp exists today because there was no room for non-Jews in the Zionist vision of creating a Jewish state. Balata was created in 1948 for thousands of Christians and Muslims expelled by Zionist forces from their homes in Jaffa, near present-day Tel Aviv. Jaffa was a major population and cultural center of Palestine until more than 66,000 residents (almost 95 percent of the population) were violently removed during Israel's creation. The "cleansing" (in the words of Zionist leaders) of the non-Jewish population of more than 500 Palestinian cities, towns, and villages like Jaffa began prior to Israel's declaration of statehood, before a single Arab soldier had set foot in the area.

I grew up believing Palestinian refugees had fled voluntarily or because of the actions of Arab regimes, but these myths have long since been debunked by Israeli and other historians. Families like Omar's were pushed to the West Bank, Gaza, and even into the sea where they were piled onto boats (an ironic reality for those who claim it is Israelis in danger of being "pushed into the sea") destined for Egypt and Lebanon. In order to create a Jewish majority where there was none before, non-Jewish families like Omar's had to be expelled.

Today—more than 60 years later—I can go to Omar's land, but he can't. Omar and 25,000 other refugees in Balata live their whole lives squeezed into a space no larger than a square kilometer and yet I, who live a life of privilege in the United States, could get Israeli citizenship and move to their land. I could live in Omar's house on his land if I wanted to, but Omar can't even visit, because he's not Jewish. This is the reality of a Jewish state—that it can only exist by denying rights to people like Omar. So what should Omar answer when asked if he recognizes such a state's right to exist? What would you and I answer in a similar situation?

Convinced that he will never be able to return to his own land, Omar wants to leave Palestine altogether. One international invited him recently to visit Germany. He applied for permission to leave but Israel rejected the application. He cannot even go to the consulate in Jerusalem because most non-Jews cannot enter the holy city. Palestinians in the Occupied Territories have no citizenship and cannot travel or migrate without permission from Israel. The police say Omar is dangerous, and I am reminded of how people become what people expect of them. I hope that Omar will be stronger than that. He said he hopes so, too.

Acknowledgments

Despite having been born in Jerusalem, I spent most of my life in the US only peripherally aware of the escalating situation in Israel/Palestine. Then, in 2002, my Israeli cousin called and asked me to translate a letter he'd written into English. In the letter, Haim (who had been an IDF commander before publicly refusing to serve) wrote that the Israeli military I'd idolized as a symbol of Jewish strength and integrity was in fact a powerful occupying force. As I translated, I digested the reality that occupation is not self-defense and that the Israeli government was suppressing the Palestinian people's freedom through inherently illegal, incredibly cruel means. For doing the right thing and for being my inspiration, I thank my cousin Haim Weiss.

Seven years later, I was lucky enough to attend a seminar by Daniel Armstrong, who challenged me to set an example for my kids by being an adult who makes her own most heartfelt dreams come true. I decided to create a book—not the kind of paid writing I'd been doing but something that came from the heart. A few weeks later I was out walking when a voice in my head (sounding just like my father, who loved walks and died in 2003) said this: "This book must be about peace." Thanks, Dad! You rarely interfered, but when you thought it was important, you were always direct and succinct in your advice.

To all my courageous, honest, gifted contributors, as well as collage artist Mim Golub Scalin and publisher Laurieann Aladin, I am full of gratitude to you for lending not only your efforts but also your hearts to *our* book.

I am extremely lucky to have friends who volunteered to proofread. Thank you Jeff Woods, Chris Ambrose, Jennifer Berry, Kathy Davies, Sara Kirshenbaum, D'Arcy Fallon, and Katy Bothwell. Thank you Clark Pendergrass for legal advice, Karen Gauthier for the maps and graph, Anis Salib for wisdom and compassion, and new friend and committed supporter Emman Chehade Randazzo.

I offer sincere gratitude to a source of inspiration and hope for many years: Jerry, the Dead, and all the creative adventurers I met along the way.

This book would never have happened without my experience at Antioch University LA, where I was mentored by nonfiction writing icons Bernard Cooper and JoAnn Beard. I also thank Dennis Covington at the University of Alabama who said, "you [pause...] are a WRITER!" Four words that gave me much-needed courage. Going back further, I would like to thank the only teacher at Brighton High who encouraged me to continue writing. You have no idea how important you were to me, Mrs. Hinkley!

Finally, I give thanks to my family. First, my sister Shira Klaiman, to whom I literally owe my sanity. For showing me what the unconditional love of parents looks like, I thank my in-laws, Stanley and Gunvor Adelfang. For teaching me to find the joy in the small things and demonstrating that the small things *are* the big things, I thank my awesome kids, Anna, Ellie, and Sasha. And for being my rockin' partner in the continuing adventure of life, Anders, I am so incredibly grateful to have you. I never dreamed it could be this good.

May peace and justice prevail.

—Osie

About the Authors

Osie Gabriel Adelfang is an Israeli-American writer and editor, part-time marketing director for her husband's design-build firm, and full-time unschooling mom of three. In a previous life, she wrote and was a copy editor for various trade magazines, corporations, nonprofits, and other clients. She also taught writing to elementary and community college students. Osie holds a BA in Journalism from the University of Massachusetts at Amherst and an MFA in creative writing from Antioch University LA. Her next project is an anthology about another topic close to her heart: older-child adoption.

Anna Baltzer is a Jewish-American Columbia graduate, former-Fulbright scholar, the granddaughter of Holocaust refugees, and an award-winning lecturer, author, and activist for Palestinian rights. As a volunteer with the International Women's Peace Service in the West Bank, Baltzer documented human rights abuses and supported Palestinian-led nonviolent resistance to the Occupation. Baltzer has appeared on television more than 100 times and lectured at more than 300 universities, schools, churches, mosques, and synagogues around the world with her acclaimed presentation, "Life in Occupied Palestine: Eyewitness Stories & Photos," and her full-color book: *Witness in Palestine: A Jewish American Woman in the Occupied Territories*. For information about Baltzer's book, DVD, speaking tours, and eye-witness reports, visit www.AnnaInTheMiddleEast.com

Over the past four decades, **Sandra Butler** has written, taught and participated in political organizing in the fields of sexual assault, breast cancer, the Jewish underpinnings of political activism, building lesbian community, Israel/Palestine, and the realities of aging. Author of *Conspiracy of Silence: The Trauma of Incest*, and co-author with Barbara Rosenblum of *Cancer in Two Voices*, Butler is the co-producer of the award-winning documentaries *Cancer in Two Voices* and *Ruthie and Connie: Every Room in the House*. She is the co-founder of Bay Area Women in Black.

Tomi Laine Clark is a wildly irreverent San Francisco-based writer who tempers her coverage of controversial topics with humor and frank honesty. Her work has appeared in *Ms. Guided* magazine, Hackwriters. com, Pology.com, *Matador Abroad*, and *Xploited*.

Born to a family rooted in the early history of the Jewish "*yishuv*," **Linda Dittmar** grew up in Tel Aviv, 1939-1960. She served in the military and studied at the Hebrew University in Jerusalem before coming to New York City. Having earned her Ph.D. from Stanford University, she taught literature and film studies at the University of Massachusetts/Boston for 40 years. Her publications include *From Hanoi to Hollywood: The Vietnam War in American Film* and *Multiple Voices in Feminist Film Criticism* as well as many articles and book chapters. She is also long-time member of the editorial board of *Radical Teacher* magazine. Much of her activism occurred in tandem with her academic work, focusing on local (US) issues such as civil rights, anti war, and gender and class struggles. In Israel she has been working with "*Zochrot*"—an organization devoted to commemorating the *Nakbah*. She is currently collaborating with a photographer on a photo-text that documents traces of Palestinian villages and the transformation of Palestinian urban life inside Israel's "green line" borders. Now Professor Emerita, she lives in Cambridge, Massachusetts.

Hedy Epstein is a Holocaust survivor, lifelong activist, and author. She has lived in the United States since 1948 and has been politically active and outspoken on the critical issues of her times, ranging from civil rights and the Viet Nam war to, more recently, the Israel/Palestine conflict. In 1999, she published her autobiography, *Erinnern ist Nicht Genug* (Remembering is not enough; Unrast Verlag, Germany). Since 2003, she has made five visits to the Israeli occupied West Bank and has spoken to various audiences in the US & around the world about her experiences. Most recently, she has become involved with the Free Gaza Movement (www.freegaza.org), attempting to break the siege by bringing Gazans humanitarian aid by boat. Hedy lives in St. Louis. She has one son and two granddaughters.

Maia Ettinger was born in Warsaw and immigrated to the United States with her mother and grandmother in 1967. A graduate of Yale College and NYU Law School, she currently is working on a novel and holds the position of legal counsel at Working Assets. She has been published in the *Berkeley Women's Law Journal* and her essay "The Pocahontas Paradigm" appeared in *Tilting the Tower*, (Routledge Press).

Kim Goldberg is the author of RED ZONE: *poems of urban decay* and five other books. Her work has appeared in numerous magazines and anthologies in North America and abroad including *The Progressive, Columbia Journalism Review, New Internationalist, Istanbul Literature Review, Voices Israel* and elsewhere. Originally from Oregon, Kim came to Canada with her family during the Vietnam War years and has lived in Nanaimo, BC, ever since. Visit: www.pigsquashpress.com

Susan Greene is an artist, educator and clinical psychologist. Her practice straddles a range of cultural arenas, new media, and public art, while focusing on borders, migrations, decolonization and memory. Greene has led or participated in more than 30 public art projects worldwide and has a research practice looking at the relationships between creativity, trauma and resilience. Greene is one of four Jewish American women artists who formed Break the Silence Mural Project in 1989. The goal of

BTS is to be a "window onto Palestine," bringing stories of life on the ground back to the USA through culture. Break the Silence artists have returned to Occupied Palestine numerous times to facilitate community mural projects, conduct arts workshops, create sculpture, make films and more. BTS' latest project is the "Olympia-Rafah Solidarity Mural Project"—an inter-disciplinary, interactive, multi-site public art project that will make use of new media and social networking technologies to increase the strength and visibility of movements organizing for social change in Palestine, Israel, the USA and the world—www.olympiara-fahmural.org, www.breakthesilencearts.org. Originally from New York City, Susan has been a resident of the Bay Area for 25 years. She teaches and directs the Learning Center at the San Francisco Art Institute and has a private psychotherapy practice.

Amira Hass is a regular columnist with Israel's Ha'aretz newspaper, and is the only Israeli journalist to have spent several years living in and reporting from Gaza and the West Bank. She is the author of *Drinking the Sea at Gaza: Days and Nights in a Land under Siege, Reporting from Ramallah: An Israeli Journalist in an Occupied Land,* and *Diary of Bergen-Belson, 1944-1945.* Hass received the 2009 Lifetime Achievement Award from the International Women's Media Foundation.

Jen Marlowe, a human rights activist, filmmaker and writer, is the founder of donkeysaddle projects. Her most recent film about South Sudan is called "Rebuilding Hope." As part of a three-person team, Jen traveled to Northern Darfur and Eastern Chad to make the documentary film "Darfur Diaries: Message from Home" and wrote the accompanying book "Darfur Diaries: Stories of Survival," which was included in the 2007 Best American Non-Required Reading edited by Dave Eggers. Jen is currently writing a play and a book about Palestine and Israel. The book is slated to be published by Nation Books in June 2010. Jen serves on the board of directors of Friends of the Jenin Freedom Theatre. Her writing can be found online at The Nation, Tomdispatch.com, Alternet, Counterpunch and CommonDreams.org.

Hannah Mermelstein is an activist and aspiring radical librarian based in Brooklyn, NY. She has lived in Palestine for more than two of the past six years, and is co-creator of Birthright Unplugged and Re-Plugged, Needle in the Groove, and Students Boycott Apartheid. In Brooklyn, Hannah works primarily with the New York Campaign for the Boycott of Israel (NYCBI) and the Palestine Education Project (PEP). She hopes to use library and archives skills to continue the search for 1948 and support the right of return for Palestinian refugees.

Emma Rosenthal is an artist, writer, educator, reiki practitioner, and human rights activist living in Southern California. Her work combines art, activism, education and grassroots mobilization. As a person with a disability, she is confined, not by her disability but by the narrow and marginalizing attitudes and structures of the society at large. Her experience as a grassroots organizer, political essayist and speaker has been life-long and has included many progressive causes. Consistent with her positions on multiculturalism and anti-imperialism, she is affirmatively Jewish and assertively anti-Zionist. In her writing, she explores the use of art and literary expression to elicit an ethos more compelling than dogma and ideological discourse, providing new paradigms for community, communion, connection and human transformation.

Alice Rothchild is an Assistant Professor of Obstetrics and Gynecology at Harvard Medical School, a contributor to the first edition of *Our Bodies, Ourselves* and author of multiple articles. She co-founded and co-chairs American Jews for a Just Peace—Boston and co-organized the AJJP Health and Human Rights Project. In April 2007, Pluto Press published her latest book, *Broken Promises, Broken Dreams: Stories of Jewish and Palestinian Trauma and Resilience*, which is distributed by Palgrave Press in the US, and she has lectured all over the US, UK, and Israel. A second edition will be released in February, 2010 with translations into Hebrew and German. She is working on a book exploring personal stories about Palestinian dispossession and expulsion as seen through the eyes of a Jewish woman well-versed in oral histories of Holocaust survivors. www.alicerothchild.com

Mim Golub Scalin (cover design) was adjunct faculty at Virginia Commonwealth University, School of the Arts, for 18 years. Currently, She teaches workshops at various venues. Educated as a painter and print-maker, she has left them to work with paper. She is currently active with mail art and small format collage pieces, weaving, stitching, and layer-ing maps, using current events printed materials, security envelopes, and photos, to make art that is personally meaningful. She has exhibited work in solo & group shows in the United States and internationally. Mim is a member of the Richmond Peace Education Center.

Cindy Sheehan, an anti-war leader after her soldier son was killed in Iraq, is credited for being one of the initial voices of protest over the Iraq war. Helping to galvanize a fledgling peace movement in the summer of 2005, Sheehan first emerged as a public figure and sparked nationwide atten-tion in August with a personal protest at the Bush ranch in Crawford, Texas. She is the author or coauthor of several books, including *Peace Mom: A Mother's Journey through Heartache to Activism, Dear President Bush,* and *Myth America.*

Starhawk, committed global justice activist and peace activist, is the author or coauthor of eleven books, including *The Spiral Dance, The Fifth Sacred Thing, Webs of Power: Notes from the Global Uprising, The Earth Path,* and the children's book *The Last Wild Witch.* She is a veteran of progressive movements, from anti-war to anti-nukes, and has made four visits to the Occupied Territories with the International Solidarity Movement. She travels globally, offering training in nonviolent direct action and permac-ulture, a system of ecological design, as well as workshop on feminist and earth-based spirituality. www.earthactivisttraining.org, www.starhawk.org

Appendix I
A Brief History

Important note: This brief timeline is intended as an overview for people unfamiliar with the Israel/Palestine conflict and is not meant to be a thorough account of the region's history.

1897: The World Zionist Organization, the first formal organization devoted to Zionism, is founded with the goal of establishing a Jewish homeland in historic Palestine (present-day Israel, the West Bank, and Gaza). At the time, Palestine is under Ottoman rule and Jews make up less than 2% of the population.

1914: Britain promises the Palestinians independence if they will lend support against Turkey in World War I.

1917: With help from the Palestinians, Britain captures Palestine from the Turks. Britain issues the Balfour Declaration endorsing the creation of a Jewish national home in Palestine, so long as it does not violate the civil and religious rights of the existing non-Jewish communities.

1920s: Following World War I, Britain receives Palestine and present-day Jordan as a mandate from the League of Nations. Palestinians oppose the idea of a Jewish state that excludes Palestinians on their land. As the Zionist movement accelerates, Palestinians protest their anticipated displacement with a general labor strike and violent attacks.

1939-1947: Jewish immigration increases in response to Nazi persecution and atrocities in Europe. In protest to British efforts to restrict immigration, Zionists organize underground gangs and launch hundreds of violent attacks against British and Palestinian officials and civilians. Palestinian opposition to Zionism continues.

1947: Britain hands the problem over to a United Nations Special Committee on Palestine, which, following pressure from the US, proposes allocating 54% of the land to Jews (who owned about 6% of the land at the time) and 46% to Palestinians (who owned or had rights to about twice that—more than 90%). Zionist leaders accept the Partition Plan publicly, although they are clear in personal correspondence that partition is only the beginning of realizing the Zionist dream encompassing all of historic Palestine (see Appendix III: Quotations). The Palestinians reject the proposal to transfer half of their land. War breaks out.

1947-1948: Recognizing the impossibility of establishing a Jewish state in a land with a non-Jewish majority, Zionist forces launch a series of operations including Plan Dalet, inducing the flight of some 750,000 Palestinians (75% of the indigenous Palestinian population). After the British pull out at the end of the mandate period, Zionists declare the State of Israel on May 15th, 1948, which becomes remembered as "Independence Day" for Jewish Israelis and the "*Nakbah*" (Catastrophe) for Palestinians.

Following the declaration and the initial expulsion of almost 300,000 Palestinians, multiple Arab countries invade the self-declared state in the second phase of the war. Israel emerges victorious and soon enacts laws officially expropriating the Palestinian refugees' property and permanently barring their return. The UN General Assembly passes Resolution 194, stating that "refugees wishing to return to their homes and live in peace with their neighbors should be permitted to do so at the earliest practicable date."

1949: The initial borders of Israel are established along what will become known as the "Green Line," encompassing 50% more territory into Israel than was originally allotted for a Jewish state by the UN Partition Plan, a total of 78% of historic Palestine. The West Bank and Gaza Strip, the remaining 22%, come under Jordanian and Egyptian control, respectively.

1950–1967: Border incidents and hostilities between Israel and surrounding countries continue.

1967: In June, Egypt blockades the Straits of Tiran. In response, Israel attacks Egypt, Syria, Iraq, and Jordan and, within six days, occupies the West Bank, Gaza Strip, Sinai Peninsula, Golan Heights, and Arab sector of East Jerusalem. About 320,000 Palestinian civilians are displaced, more than half of them for the second time. Israel immediately begins establishing Jewish-only settlements in the West Bank, Gaza, and East Jerusalem.

In November, the UN Security Council passes Resolution 242, stressing the "inadmissibility of the acquisition of territory by war" and calling for the "withdrawal of Israeli armed forces from territories occupied," affirming the necessity for "freedom of navigation through international waterways" and "a just settlement to the refugee problem." Israel maintains positions in the Occupied Territories and prevents the old and new refugees from returning to their homes.

1973: On the Jewish holy day of Yom Kippur in October, Egypt and Syria attack Israeli positions in the occupied Sinai and Golan Heights. With significant US economic and military assistance, Israel succeeds in forcing the Egyptians and Syrians back.

1979: Having suffered heavy losses there during the 1973 War, Israel returns the Sinai to Egypt in exchange for normal diplomatic relations with Egypt and Israeli access to the Suez Canal.

1980: The Israeli Knesset (Parliament) adopts the Jerusalem Law, officially annexing East Jerusalem into Israel.

1981: Israel accelerates the establishment of Jewish-only settlements in Occupied Territories and officially annexes the Golan Heights.

1987–1993: The first major Palestinian uprising against the Occupation begins, continuing for six years. Known as the First Intifada, it is largely nonviolent. The Israeli military response is harsh. For example, Defense Minister Yitzhak Rabin (who would later become Israeli Prime Minister) orders soldiers to break the bones of Palestinian youth. Many of the tens of thousands injured are under ten.

1988: Yasser Arafat, the top representative of the Palestinian people, officially recognizes Israel's right to exist and renounces violence.

1993–1996: Israeli and Palestinian representatives sign the Oslo Accords, granting Palestinian complete control over 3% of the West Bank (.6% of historic Palestine), shared control over 27%, and complete Israeli control over the remaining 70%, with the expectation of the withdrawal of Israeli troops from Gaza and most West Bank cities and towns. Negotiations over remaining issues are planned to follow withdrawal and a five-year transitional period. Israel doesn't withdraw troops and embarks on an accelerated settlement program, building thousands of new housing units in the West Bank and doubling the settler population during the transitional period.

1994: A Jewish American settler in Hebron massacres 29 Palestinians praying in a mosque. Israeli troops place Hebron Palestinians, but not the settlers, under curfew. Shortly thereafter, the first Palestinian suicide bomber blows himself up inside Israel. Brutal attacks against Israelis continue until the present, often correlating with Israeli brutality in the Occupied Territories.

2000: Negotiations for a final settlement at Camp David II are unsuccessful. Sharon's September visit to the Temple Mount with 1,000 soldiers sparks riots that escalate into the Second Intifada. By the end of the year, 42 Israelis and 327 Palestinians have been killed.

2001: Negotiations at Taba are unsuccessful. Violence from both sides surges in the Occupied Territories. Over the course of the year, 190 Israelis and 577 Palestinians are killed.

2002: The Arab League, composed of 22 Arab countries, proposes peace, normal relations, and regional integration with Israel in exchange for an end to the Occupation and a "just solution" to the refugee problem. Israel rejects the offer and begins unilateral construction of the Wall. Over the course of the year, 422 Israelis and 1072 Palestinians are killed.

2003–2004: The "Quartet" (U.S., UN, EU, and Russia) develop a "Roadmap to Peace." The Palestinians pledge full support; Israel rejects key sections. Over the course of both years, 295 Israelis and 1,547 Palestinians are killed.

2005: Israel evacuates 8,000 settlers from Gaza, meanwhile constructing new housing units for 13,000 more settlers in the West Bank. Israeli troops withdraw from Gaza but retain control of free-fire zones with snipers, as well as crossings, airspace, and coastline.

2006: Hamas defeats Fatah in the democratic legislative elections after holding to a unilateral ceasefire for more than one year. The US and EU cut off aid and declare an embargo on the Palestinian government, on which Palestinian civil society is dependent. Poverty soars to unprecedented levels. Interfactional violence breaks out between Hamas and Fatah.

In June, two days after Israeli soldiers capture two Palestinians in Gaza, Gaza militants kill two Israeli soldiers and capture one. Israel launches a five-month attack on Gaza leaving eight Israelis (two of them civilians) and 400 Palestinians (mostly civilians) dead. Hamas temporarily breaks its unilateral ceasefire in June but quickly resumes it, even as the bombardment of Gaza continues. The US and Israel begin arming and training Fatah soldiers to overthrow the elected government.

2007: Anticipating the coup, Hamas leaders seize control of the Gaza Strip, the population of which had elected them. Interfactional violence intensifies in the Hamas-controlled Gaza Strip and Fatah-controlled West Bank.

Israel maintains control over Gaza's borders, airspace, and shores. Israel and Egypt blockade the strip, crippling the economy and preventing inhabitants from receiving basic needs, including adequate food, water, and medicine. Israeli air strikes, incursions, and extrajudicial assassinations of Gaza residents continue. Hamas starts launching homemade rockets into Southern Israel, causing damage but no casualties.

2008: In June, Hamas and Israel declare a six-month ceasefire. Israel agrees to ease the blockade if Hamas ceases rocket attacks. In November, Israel officially violates the ceasefire in a cross-border raid and air strike, killing six Hamas members. Hamas responds with a wave of rockets into the Southern Israel. Small-scale violence continues on both sides and in late December, Israel begins a 22-day large-scale invasion and aerial bombardment of the Gaza Strip called "Operation Cast Lead," planned months in advance. Hamas continues firing homemade rockets.

2009: Operation Cast Lead ends with deaths on both sides: 13 Israelis (including three civilians and four soldiers killed by friendly fire) and 1,400 Palestinians (including 926 civilians). One third of Gaza's agricultural is destroyed and close to 100,000 Palestinians are left homeless.

Israel's blockade of Gaza continues throughout the year, cutting off Palestinians from adequate food, water, medicine, electricity, or materials to rebuild their homes and lives. Palestinians wishing to enter or leave Gaza to be with their families or attend universities are systematically denied permits. Israeli settlement construction persists. Violence on both sides continues.

Sources: Jimmy Carter, *Palestine: Peace Not Apartheid* (New York: Simon & Schuster, 2006) and Benny Morris, *The Birth of the Palestinian Refugee Problem* (Cambridge University Press, 1988), plus online sources: *Haaretz Israeli Newspaper, Columbia Encyclopedia, BBC, CBC News, Amnesty International, Human Rights Watch, MIFTAH, Christian Century, Jerusalem Fund, PalestineHistory.com, Double Standards Palestine and Israel Timeline,* and *Middle East Policy Council.*

Appendix II Maps

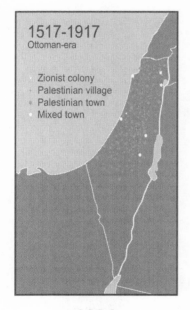

1517-1917
Ottoman-era

- Zionist colony
- Palestinian village
- Palestinian town
- Mixed town

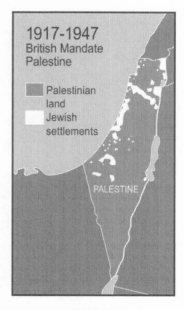

1917-1947
British Mandate
Palestine

- Palestinian land
- Jewish settlements

PALESTINE

1881

- Palestinian population (442,000)
- Jewish population (25,000)

5%
95%

1922

- Palestinian population (723,000)
- Jewish population (93,000)

11%
89%

1947
UN Partition Plan

Jewish state

Palestinian
state

Jerusalem
(UN Admin)

1949-1967
Armistice Line

Israel

Palestinian
land

under Jordanian rule

under Egyptian rule

ISRAEL

1950

- Palestinian, in "green line Israel" (159,000)
- Jewish (1,203,000)
- in West Bank (765,00)
- in Gaza (240,000)

10% 7%

32% 51%

1967 Israel
(Israel occupies West Bank, Gaza, Sinai, and Golan Heights and annexes East Jerusalem)

☐ Israeli Land

▨ '67 Israeli Occupation

ISRAEL

1967

■ Palestinian, in
"green line Israel" (393,000)
■ Jewish (2,384,000)
■ in West Bank (677,00)
■ in Gaza (368,000)

10%   10%
18%
62%

1990

■ Palestinian, in
"green line Israel" (875,000)
■ Jewish (3,947,000)
■ in West Bank (1,255,00)
■ in Gaza (643,000)

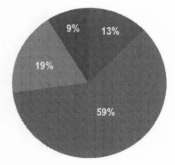

9%   13%
19%
59%

2006

- ■ Palestinian, in
  "green line Israel" (1,413,000)
- ■ Jewish (5,393,000)
- ■ in West Bank (2,400,00)
- ■ in Gaza (1,380,000)

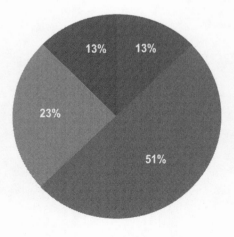

Appendix III
Quotations from Prominent Figures

EARLY ZIONIST LEADERS ON THE
FULFILLMENT OF ZIONISM

We shall try to spirit the penniless population across the border by procuring employment for them in the transit countries while denying any employment in our country. Both the process of expropriation and the removal of the poor must be carried out discretely and circumspectly.[1]

—THEODOR HERZL, the founder of Zionism, 1897

We must expel the Arabs and take their places and if we have to use force to guarantee our own right to settle in those places—then we have force at our disposal.[2]

—DAVID BEN-GURION,
Israel's founding father and first prime minister, 1937

---

1   Raphael Patai, *The Complete Diaries of Theodor Herzl* (New York, 1961), p. 88; As cited in Finkelstein, *Image*, p. 176, footnote 19.

2   Nur Masalha, *Expulsion of Palestinians*, p. 66; As cited in "What leading Israelis have said about the Nakba," *Institute for Middle East Understanding* (May 9, 2007).

In Palestine we do not propose to go through the form of consulting the wishes of the present inhabitants... The four great powers are committed to Zionism and Zionism, be it right or wrong, good or bad, is rooted in age-long tradition, in present needs, in future hopes, of far profounder import than the desires and prejudices of the 700,000 Arabs who now inhabit that ancient land.[3]

—LORD BALFOUR,
British Foreign Secretary, author of the *Balfour Declaration*,
promising a "homeland for the Jews" in Palestine, 1919

Zionist colonization, even the most restricted, must either be terminated or carried out in defiance of the will of the native population.[4]

—VLADIMIR JABOTINSKY,
founder of revisionist Zionism, 1923

I support compulsory transfer. I do not see in it anything immoral... The Arabs will have to go, but one needs an opportune moment for making it happen, such as a war.[5]

—DAVID BEN-GURION,
Israel's founding father and first prime minister, 1937

DURING THE WAR OF 1948

In the Negev we will not buy land. We will conquer it.[6]

—DAVID BEN-GURION,
Israel's founding father and first prime minister

---

3   Edward Said, *The Question of Palestine*; As cited in *The Origin of the Palestine-Israel Conflict*, published by Jews for Justice in the Middle East, third edition.

4   Vladimir Jabotinsky, *The Iron Wall: We and the Arabs*; As cited in Qumsiyeh, p. 75.

5   Ilan Pappe, *The Ethnic Cleansing of Palestine* (Oxford: Oneworld Publications, 2006).

6   Benny Morris, *The Birth of the Palestinian Refugee Problem, 1947-1949* (Cambridge, 1988), p. 170.

These operations can be carried out in the following manner: either by destroying villages (by setting fire to them, by blowing them up, and by planting mines in their rubble), and especially those population centers that are difficult to control permanently; or by mounting combing and control operations according to the following guidelines: encirclement of the villages, conducting a search inside them. In case of resistance, the armed forces must be wiped out and the population expelled outside the borders of the state.[7]

—From Operation Dalet, adopted by the Zionist leadership in 1948

[Capturing the village] without a fight, [Zionist forces first] killed about 80-100 [male] Arabs, women and children. The children they killed by breaking their heads with sticks. There was not a house without dead... One soldier boasted that he had raped a woman and then shot her. One woman, with a newborn baby in her arms, was employed to clear the courtyard where the soldiers ate. She worked a day or two. In the end they shot her and her baby.[8]

—Eyewitness soldier of the massacre at
Ad-Dawayima village in October of 1948

EARLY ZIONIST LEADERS ON PARTITION

The debate has not been for or against the indivisibility of Eretz Israel [the "Land of Israel," including the West Bank and Gaza]. No Zionist can forgo the smallest portion of Eretz Israel. The debate was over which of two routes would lead quicker to the common goal.[9]

I have no doubt that our army will be among the world's outstanding—and so I am certain that we won't be constrained from settling in the rest of the country, whether out of accord and mutual understanding with the Arab neighbors or otherwise.[10]

---

7   The English translation is in Walid Khalidi, "Plan Dalet: Master Plan for the Conquest of Palestine," Journal of Palestine Studies, issue 1 (1988), pp. 4-20; As cited in Pappe, "The 1948 Ethnic Cleansing of Palestine," Journal of Palestine Studies, issue 141 (2006).

8   Morris, p. 230; As cited in Finkelstein, Image, p. 76.

9   Quote from 1937. Arlosoroff memorandum; As cited in Chomsky, Fateful, p. 162.

10 Yosef Gorny, Zionism and the Arabs, 1882-1948: A Study of Ideology (Oxford: Clarendon, 1987), p. 260; As cited and expanded in Finkelstein, Image, p. 15.

After the formation of a large army in the wake of the establishment of the state, we will abolish partition and expand to the whole of Palestine.[11]

—DAVID BEN-GURION,
Israel's founding father and first prime minister, 1937

The partition of the Homeland is illegal. It will never be recognized... It will not bind the Jewish people. Jerusalem was and will forever be our capital. Eretz Israel [the "Land of Israel," including the West Bank and Gaza] will be restored to the people of Israel. All of it. And forever.[12]

—MENACHEM BEGIN, 6th Israeli Prime Minister, 1954

AFTER THE ESTABLISHMENT OF ISRAEL

In our country there is room only for the Jews. We shall say to the Arabs: Get out! If they don't agree, if they resist, we shall drive them out by force.[13]

—BEN-ZION DINUR, Israeli Minister of Education and Culture, 1954

Why should the Arabs make peace? If I was an Arab leader, I would never make terms with Israel. That is natural: we have taken their country. Sure, God promised it to us, but what does that matter to them?... They only see one thing: we have come here and stolen their country. Why should they accept that? They may perhaps forget in one or two generations' time, but for the moment there is no chance. [14]

—DAVID BEN-GURION,
Israel's founding father and first prime minister, 1956

---

11 Quote from 1937. Remi Kanazi, "Transferring the Truth," *AIC* (September 20, 2005).

12 Menachem Begin, "The Revolt" (New York: Schuman, 1951), p. 335; As cited in Chomsky, *Fateful*, p. 161

13 *History of the Haganah*; As cited in Sam Bahour, "Israel at 58: A Failed Experiment," *Electronic Intifada* (May 15, 2006).

14 Nahum Goldmann, *The Jewish Paradox* (New York: Grosset & Dunlap, 1978); As cited in *The Origin of the Palestine-Israel Conflict*, published by Jews for Justice in the Middle East, third edition.

LEADING UP TO THE 1967 WAR AND THE OCCUPATION

[Israel must] invent dangers, and to do this it must adopt the method of provocation-and-revenge... And above all—let us hope for a new war with the Arab countries, so that we may finally get rid of our troubles and acquire our space.[15]

—MOSHE SHARATT, Israeli Prime Minister in 1953-1955

In the case of the new war, we must avoid the historic mistake of the War of Independence [1948 War] and, later, the Sinai Campaign. We must not cease fighting until we achieve... the territorial fulfillment of the Land of Israel.[16]

—YIGAL ALLON, Interim Prime Minister in 1969, Architect of the Allon Plan

REFLECTIONS ON THE 1967 WAR

I do not think that Nasser wanted war. The two divisions he sent to the Sinai would not have been sufficient to launch an offensive war. He knew it and we knew it.[17]

—YITZHAK RABIN, Israel's 5th Prime Minister, 1968

In June 1967, we again had a choice. The Egyptian Army concentrations in the Sinai approaches do not prove that Nasser was really about to attack us. We must be honest with ourselves. We decided to attack him.[18]

—Menachem Begin, 6TH ISRAELI PRIME MINISTER, 1982

---

15 Livia Rokach, *Israel's Sacred Terrorism* (AAUG Press, 1986); As cited in *The Origin of the Palestine-Israel Conflict*, published by Jews for Justice in the Middle East, third edition.

16 Michael Brecher, *Decisions in Crisis* (Berkeley: 1980), p. 100; As cited in Finkelstein, *Image*, pp. 195-196.

17 *Le Monde* (February 28, 1968); As cited in *The Origin of the Palestine-Israel Conflict*, published by Jews for Justice in the Middle East, third edition.

18 "Address by Prime Minister Begin at the National Defense College," *Israeli Ministry of Foreign Affairs* (August 8, 1982).

I know how at least 80 percent of all the incidents with Syria started. In my opinion, more than 80 percent... It would go like this: we would send a tractor to plow... in the demilitarized area, and we would know ahead of time that the Syrians would start shooting. If they did not start shooting, we would inform the tractor to progress further, until the Syrians, in the end, would get nervous and would shoot. And then we would use guns, and later, even the air force, and that is how it went... We thought... that we could change the lines of the cease-fire accords by military actions that were less than a war. That is, to seize some territory and hold it until the enemy despairs and gives it to us.[19]

—MOSHE DAYAN, Israeli Defense Minister, 1976

QUOTES FROM MODERN ISRAELI LEADERS

It is the duty of Israeli leaders to explain to public opinion, clearly and courageously, a certain number of facts that are forgotten with time. The first of these is no Zionism, colonialization [sic], or Jewish State without the eviction of the Arabs and the expropriation of their lands.[20]

Everybody has to move, run and grab as many hilltops as they can to enlarge the settlements because everything we take now will stay ours... Everything we don't grab will go to them.[21]

—ARIEL SHARON, Israeli Prime Minister from 2001 to 2006

The vision I would like to see here is the entrenching of the Jewish and the Zionist state... I very much favor democracy, but when there is a contradiction between democratic and Jewish values, the Jewish and Zionist values are more important.[22]

—AVIGDOR LIEBERMAN, Israeli Minister of Strategic Threats, 2006

---

19 "Interviews on the Golan Heights and on Jewish Settlements in Hebron," *Yediot Ahronot* (November 22, 1976); As cited in Finkelstein, Image, p. 187.

20 Agence French Presse (November 15, 1998); As cited in "What leading Israelis have said about the Nakba," *Institute for Middle East Understanding* (May 9, 2007).

21 Quote from 1998. Ibid, at 147.

22 Scotsman (October 23, 2006); As cited in Ali Abunimah, "World silent as fascists join Israeli government," *Electronic Intifada* (October 25, 2006).

FORMER ISRAELI LEADER ON JEWISH RESISTANCE TO BRITISH OCCUPATION

Neither Jewish ethics nor Jewish tradition can disqualify terrorism as a means of combat... First and foremost, terrorism is for us a part of the political battle being conducted under the present circumstances, and it has a great part to play... in our war against the occupier.[23]

—YITZHAK SHAMIR, 7th Israeli Prime Minister

MODERN ISRAELI HISTORIAN ON THE DISCREPANCY BETWEEN THE COLLECTIVE UNDERSTANDING AND THE REALITY ILLUSTRATED BY THESE CANDID QUOTATIONS

When it comes to the dispossession by Israel of the Palestinians in 1948, there is a deep chasm between the reality and the representation. This is most bewildering, and it is difficult to understand how events perpetrated in modern times and witnessed by foreign reporters and UN observers could be systematically denied, not even recognized as historical fact, let alone acknowledged as a crime that needs to be confronted, politically as well as morally. Nonetheless, there is no doubt that the ethnic cleansing of 1948, the most formative event in the modern history of the land of Palestine, has been almost entirely eradicated from the collective global memory and erased from the world's conscience.[24]

—ILAN PAPPE, prominent Israeli "New Historian," 2006

---

23 Yitzhak Shamir, *Hehazit*, LEHI, the "Stern Gang" (1943); translated in *Middle East Report* (1988); As cited in Chomsky, Fateful, pp. 485-486.

24 Ilan Pappe, "The 1948 Ethnic Cleansing of Palestine," *Journal of Palestine Studies*, issue 141 (2006).

GANDHI ON PALESTINIAN RESISTANCE

I am not defending the Arab excesses. I wish they had chosen the way of non-violence in resisting what they rightfully regard as an unacceptable encroachment upon their country. But according to the accepted canons of right and wrong, nothing can be said against the Arab resistance in the face of overwhelming odds.[25]

—MAHATMA GANDHI

---

25 Martin Buber and Paul R. Mendes-Flohr, *A Land of Two Peoples* (University of Chicago Press, 2005); As cited in *The Origin of the Palestine-Israel Conflict*, published by Jews for Justice in the Middle East, third edition.

Appendix IV
Facts and Figures

Casualties and material losses from
September 28, 2000 - March 2, 2010

Total number of Palestinian deaths: 7346
    Children: 1289
    Women: 581
    Men: 5476

Palestinians killed by Jewish settlers: 80
Palestinians killed as a result of Israeli shelling: 2913
Deaths as a result of preventing medical personnel
at Israeli checkpoints: 401
Stillbirths (Palestinian babies born dead at checkpoints): 32

Number of Palestinians extra-judicially killed and assassinated: 836
    Bystanders killed during extra-judicial killings: 353

Total number Israeli deaths: 1676
    Children: 123
    Women: 306
    Men: 642

Settlers:..236
Soldiers: 345

Area distribution of Palestinian deaths:
West Bank (including east Jerusalem): 2116
Gaza Strip: 5062

Palestinians injured by Israeli forces and settlers: 50615
Live ammunition:..9118
Rubber-coated steel bullets:.. 17242
Tear gas: 6895
Miscellaneous: 17360

Number of Palestinians permanently disabled or
maimed by injuries:..3634

Education Statistics:
School students killed: 925
Injured: 4100
Detained: 932

University students killed:..200
Injured: 1245
Detained: 720

Teachers killed: 37
Injured: 55
Detained: 190

Destruction of Palestinian property in dunums (1 dunum = 1000 square
meters)
Confiscated land: 272078
Razed land: 80481
Estimated number of uprooted trees:...................................1191463
Homes demolished: 10402

Sources:
[1]: The Palestinian Central Bureau of Statistics (PCBS)
  * main source

[2]: Palestinian Ministry of Education and Higher Education

[3]: Applied Research Institute Jerusalem (ARIJ)

[4]: Palestinian Red Crescent Society (PRCS)

[5]: Palestinian Centre for Human Rights (PCHR)

[6]: Palestine Monitor

[7]: International Solidarity Movement

(Fact sheet reprinted with permission from MIFTAH.ORG, The Palestinian Initiative for the Promotion of Global Dialogue & Democracy)

Appendix V
Get Involved!

What Can You Do?
Here are a few things you can do
to help bring change to Israel/Palestine.

1. **Do Your Own Research.** Go beyond mainstream media sources (which enforce a virtual blackout on information favorable to Palestinians or critical of the Israeli government). Some sources of information to start with include:
   - www.haaretz.com (Israeli newspaper)
   - english.aljazeera.net
   - www.al-awda.org
   - www.IfAmericansKnew.org
   - www.electronicintifada.net
   - www.alternativenews.org
   - www.palestinechronicle.com
   - www.pij.org
   - www.btselem.org

   You will find more information as you continue to research and will become more discerning as to whether a site or other media source is displaying propaganda or factual information.

But remember that knowledge about Palestine is meaningless if you don't use it. Palestinians don't need more people feeling sorry for them; they need people to take action. Don't put off acting until you know everything—you never will. Keep researching as you take some of the following actions!

2. **Join a Local Group.** Solidarity groups for peace and justice are organizing worldwide. Many US groups are listed at www.endtheoccupation.org and www.unitedforpeace.org. Many groups in Canada are listed at www.caiaweb.org. If there's no group in your area, you can always start one. Whether you're part of a group or on your own, there are many ways to take action. Whatever your group does, if you are in the US, make sure you join the *US Campaign to End the Israeli Occupation*, the umbrella organization for Palestine solidarity groups that provides support for groups doing all of the above around the country. Visit www.endtheoccupation.org.

3. **Join the Boycott, Divestment, and Sanctions (BDS) Campaign against Israel.** When Palestinians were asked what they most wanted from the international supporters, they called for boycott, divestment, and sanctions against Israel until it complies with international law. BDS is a nonviolent way for the international community to mobilize and put pressure on Israel in a style similar to that used against South Africa to help end Apartheid there. Read the Palestinian call, FAQs, examples of campaigns and successes, and much more at www.bdsmovement.net to help you get started. For a list of companies profiting in different ways from the oppression of Palestinians: www.InterfaithPeaceInitiative.com/profitingfromoccupation.htm

4. **Hold Educational Events.** Invite speakers or screen a film. There's a Speakers Bureau at www.palestinefreedom.org/?q=speakers and film ideas at www.palestineonlinestore.com/films/index.html. You can then air taped events and films on local Public Access TV. Contact Whole World Press if you are interested in hearing more from the editor or contributors to *Shifting Sands* (www.wholeworldpress.org).

5. **Write to and/or Meet with your Local Representatives.** For US groups, the US Campaign (information below) and the American Association for Palestinian rights at www.aaper.org offer support to help individuals and groups lobby for a responsible and just foreign policy in Palestine.

6. **Monitor The Media.** If you notice biased coverage in local or national media (or, just as likely, no coverage when important events are going on in Palestine), write op-eds or letters to the editor and call TV or talk radio stations to let them know you expect the full story. This strategy is most effective when we act together. Join the WRITE! Project at www.writetruth.org to get alerts about media letter-writing campaigns.

7. **Go to Palestine.** It will change your life. Just being there in solidarity and sharing your experiences with people back home is one of the most effective actions you can take. You can go as a solidarity volunteer, with a delegation, or just to tour and see for yourself. Anna Baltzer's website, www.annainthemiddleeast.com/findoutmore/index.html includes a list of organizations through which you can visit Palestine.

The information in this index was researched and contributed by Anna Baltzer. More detailed information can be found in her book, Witness in Palestine, as well as on her website: www.AnnaInTheMiddleEast.com/whatcanyou/index.html

5367178R0

Made in the USA
Lexington, KY
01 May 2010